Little Boygium

by

Joel Savage

"Little Boygium," by Joel Savage. ISBN 978-1-62137-238-7 (softcover); 978-1-62137-239-4 (Ebook).

Published 2013 by Virtualbookworm.com Publishing Inc., P.O. Box 9949, College Station, TX 77842, US.

Manufactured in the United States of America.

Dedication

Dedicated to Jethrol Savage

I am indebted to many of my Belgian friends for sharing many important issues with me. Finally my thanks to Musah Ibrahim Musah (African News Analysis). I appreciate all the help in making this publication possible.

Table of Contents

Preface

In every country, there is a monument or symbol which brings immediate familiarity, attention, or recognition to that country; The Statue of Liberty represents America, the Eiffel tower is France pride, the Colosseum explores Italy's bloodiest history, and the statue of Jesus Christ is Brazil's redeemer. Belgium's representational monument is the 'Mannek en Pis'. This popular statue of a little boy urinating was made by Hierronymus Duquesnoy in 1619 and has stolen the heart of many tourists worldwide.

Because of the statue's popularity in Belgium, the writer chose to name his fifth memoire *Little Boygium*. As an immigrant from an English speaking country trying to integrate into a Belgian society that has Flemish, French and German as the official languages was a nightmare. The writer wanted to further his education in journalism but he couldn't because the courses were only offered in Netherlands and French at higher institutions in Antwerp.

To survive as an immigrant, pay his rent, and cater to the welfare of his family, Joel had no choice but to attend a forklift driving school. Unfortunately, completing driving school didn't help him, since he couldn't get a permanent job as a forklift driver. When forklift driving didn't work out, he found his permanent job as a full time cleaner. Joel once said that "cleaners are human beings too who deserve to be respected. They brighten the environment and prevent the outbreak of epidemic. I don't want foreign language to be a barrier. It's my goal, desire, and ambition to follow my passion as a writer, and; barriers don't matter to me."

After finishing his cleaning job at the school for the day, Joel would sit for hours behind his computer at home writing three books at the same time. This was a hard period that he calls the "Wonderful Experience." This book describes the rough road Joel travelled while becoming a writer, working at a job where he was the subject of ridicule and laughter for trying to raise funds to support the publication of his books. He commented that "I found it weird when some of the teachers laughed at me. Even though I felt the impact, it didn't break me down. It encouraged me to write this book instead."

Little Boygium, Wonderful Experience is an interesting book of inspiration and encouragement for anyone whom may suddenly find themselves in an entirely different environment and career. It is a book that represents a way to get away from frustration, depression, anxiety, and hopelessness. There is nothing more satisfying in life than when you find a solution for your desperate situation. Get the teachings from this book.

New in Belgium

Like many immigrants, I asked to stay in Belgium through the request of political asylum. As a naturalised national of the Republic of Sierra Leone, I came with genuine documents which helped and facilitated my application. They were naturally precautious because, much like Rwanda, blood was flowing in Sierra Leone as a result of a brutal civil war. The man who interviewed me was an expert. He was an intelligent man who knew much about African affairs. I felt very proud of him for being a white man with immense knowledge of Africa. I sat in front of him and read boldly what was written in front of his t-shirt: "AFRICA."

Interviews make many people nervous, because one doesn't know the questions to be asked, even if you have an idea about the subject. Despite that, I was fully prepared. When the interview began, the questions weren't easy. If I had not been from Sierra Leone or had no knowledge of the country, I would have failed the interview miserably and lost my opportunity to live in Belgium. The interviewer was extremely intelligent. I don't know how many times he had visited Africa or

Sierra Leone, but the questions aimed at me clearly revealed that he had previously visited other African countries, including Sierra Leone.

Many of the dozens of questions were focused on the country and the people, particularly the Mende, Susu, Fula, Temne, Limba and the Creole. The Creole were the people who took the pidgin English or Patois dialect as a means of communication when they first set their feet ashore Freetown as descendants of freed slaves and settled at the place which later became the capital. My final question was "At the Siaka Stevens Street, there was a roundabout, which the Creole people usually called 'Turntable.' The famous circular road is called 'Sakula road.' Inside the roundabout stands an object. What is that object?" "The famous cotton tree," I answered. The cotton tree is an historical symbol of Freetown since 1792.

At the end of the interview, he asked me if I wanted something to drink and I requested a glass of water. He rose from behind his desk and went to get a glass of water for me. I emptied the whole glass into my stomach, because the interview had made me very thirsty. I still don't know how he knew that. After I drank the water, he asked me a question that I remember better than any of the other questions he had asked me. "If you are granted a stay in Belgium, would you like to work?"

"I don't know if I will live in Belgium, but if I will, I'm going to work very hard," I answered and he smiled. I was shown to a very big hall to wait for my result. It was a frightening experience, indeed.

In the same big hall, there were hundreds of other asylum seekers from various countries all awaiting their fates. Some were sad or crying while others were disoriented or mentally disturbed. Surprisingly, there were many Sierra Leoneans whose applications were rejected. The Belgian authorities were doing their job well. Some of the Sierra Leoneans failed to even answer simple questions or explain their country of origin fully. A white European could describe Africa better than some of the people of my country. I was disturbed.

I had already spent nearly three and a half hours at the big hall, by the time I heard my name called. I went to the man who had called out to me and he handed me some papers. I passed my interview and was declared positive. I had cleared the biggest hurdle. I then returned to the Red Cross centre, where I was living with many refugees. There, I enrolled in a Netherlands class to learn the language. It was interesting to learn a language with different people from various countries. I didn't realize the number of Europeans that also request political asylum, until I lived at that refugee house. There were many Europeans there that came from some of the most broken states in Russia and Eastern Europe.

I was there for exactly six weeks until I moved to live in Antwerp. I chose to live in Antwerp because it has one of the largest, busiest seaports in the world. After growing up in a coastal environment, I was thrilled to live by the sea again. But, the morning before I left the centre for the last time, the Red Cross administration received a family from Russia. They were a mother, a twenty-year-old son, and a daughter of eighteen, accompanied by three heavy travelling suitcases. They looked better than the refugees fleeing persecution normally looked. I thought it's likely that they were migrating from Russia to have a good taste of Belgium delicacies, chocolates, and quality beers.

One of the Red Cross staff who attended school in Russia could speak and write Russian. She was called in to interview the family. Normally, refugees under investigation at the request of asylum were brought to live at the centre by the Belgium authorities until the investigations were completed but this Russian family came directly to the Red Cross centre. During the interview, those who could speak and understand Russian were standing in front of the administration office laughing uncontrollably. I tried to find out why everyone was laughing at the family, but no one responded immediately. Then the family was given a room and an appointment with the authorities in Brussels.

After the family left, one of those laughing told me that the mother of the children told the Red Cross staff that someone told them to migrate to Belgium because the Belgian O.C.M.W. would give them money every month to live better than they did in Russia. They had already failed their initial interview for migrating to Belgium as economic refugees. I now knew the reason people who understood the language were laughing.

The 'Openbaar Centrum Maatschappelijk Welzijn' or the O.C.M.W that the woman mentioned was a social welfare centre that unknowingly made many financial mistakes that affected their future. As a social welfare centre that provided social services for the well-being of every Belgian citizen, they gave money to jobless individuals, but they didn't put pressure on the citizens to find jobs. The organisation offered financial help, accommodation, medical assistance and jobs for many unemployed, but took too many people with insufficient income into consideration.

Even though the organisation investigated the situation or resources of all applicants before giving assistance, they made many grave mistakes which have presently created a deep financial crisis. The misappropriation of funds and blunders committed by the O.C.M.W can never be rectified. Today, they are facing a terribly unanticipated financial crisis. Some of the people they assisted, even those that were not disabled, completely refused to look for a job because the financial assistance provided them with all the money they needed. The social company would assist an unemployed individual with 900 Euros monthly, and since they would likely only earn 1100 Euros if they worked, they would simply choose to not work at all. Without pressure from the O.C.M.W, many people remained on the social list for years, enjoying and living on the taxpayers' money.

Another mistake the Belgian authorities made was keeping many of the refugees on the waiting list for two to four years, leaving them to depend fully on the benefits of the O.C.M.W, without given them papers to work. At one time, there were refugees, who had requested for political asylum, living better than some of the hard-working Belgian citizens. Just imagine asylum seekers, saving enough money to buy cars and driving through the city, wasting fuel that many of the hard working citizens couldn't afford.

As a newcomer in Antwerp, I noticed this problem early on but assumed that the authorities simply accepted it. Refugees without working permits were driving, but they avoided the expensive practical driving cost and theory examination so the simple method to get them behind the steering-wheel was to go to the municipal to change their driving licences. There were specific countries in which drivers licenses could easily be changed.

Then false drivers licenses began pouring in and the licence changing procedure was soon cancelled.

The ignorance amongst many Africans can be large indeed. In Africa, many things go on without the authorities doing anything about the problems. This ignorance came along with some of them when they migrated to Europe. Many Africans drive without drivers licences even though they were aware of the dangers and the penalty that comes from driving without a licence. There were many accidents in the city involving foreigners and the police arrested and impounded many vehicles as a measure to prevent any further calamity or accident.

Every country in Europe has its plan on how to control its citizens and foreigners. I think Belgium's plan is simply the best amongst the plans in Europe. I rented a single bedroom apartment in Antwerp after leaving the Red Cross Centre and after registering at the commune or municipal, I was told that the police would come to see if I lived at the address I provided. When enforced by the Belgian authorities, this plan has made Belgium freer from crime than most European countries. But waiting for the police took longer than expected. Without any friends or any place to go, it was like living in solitary confinement. I would sit the whole day, waiting for the police to come, ascertain my presence, and give me a signed document for the commune so that I could get my initial papers of stay. I waited for days and the police still hadn't come.

I was told that the police would come any moment uninformed. Sometimes they would come when the foreigner wasn't home and send a report that the individual isn't residing there, which could cost you your legal resident papers. Knowing this, I could not even use the bathroom comfortably. I constantly listened for a knock at the door. I waited in that house for two months. Whenever I went to the supermarket, I would paste a notice on the door letting them know that I was off to the supermarket. One day while I was at the supermarket, I saw two policemen driving around the neighbourhood and I stopped them because I thought they had been to my place. After identifying myself and telling them the reason I stopped them, they told me that "it's the area police responsible for that job."

The day the policeman came was like witnessing a miracle. I was extremely happy. Seeing the policeman was the first happiness I tasted in Belgium. I told him how long I had been waiting for him and he replied that he had been on holiday. It took precisely three months before I saw his face. Imagine being in a house for three months and going nowhere but the supermarket. He gave me the signed papers and asked me to go to the foreigner's office to begin the process of my initial papers. It was raining heavily when I left home and I didn't even wait for it to stop. I went on because I was tired of being at home after that agonising three months.

At foreigners' office in Antwerp, I witnessed a shocking scene that imprinted itself in my mind. A crowd of mostly foreigners were waiting outside the closed door after being denied access inside the office, because they ignored instructions when directed to form a queue. It was still raining and they were all wet from head to toe, standing there while the workers laughed at them from the windows above. I found the situation very disturbing. The police came to try and organise them, but the angry wet crowd refused to pay any attention so the police left the scene. I stood there in the pouring rain for two hours. Finally, I could no longer ignore the locked door and my drenched clothes, so I decided to return home.

I had an opportunity to enter into the office on the third day to file my papers. At the table, I asked the woman assisting me the reason they shut us out that day. She told me that every foreigner wants to live in Antwerp, which has caused many of problems for them. There were only four workers there to serve hundreds of refugees each day. I then realised that they acted callously to satisfy their anger and frustration. At least, I finally had my initial documents of stay. The search for the job continued.

Belgium, the People, the Education

Belgium is a relatively a small country compared to the other European countries. As a federal state, the country is divided into three regions: the Dutch-Flemish occupying the north, the Francophone-Walloons in the South and the capital, Brussels, plus a small group of Germans, in the East. Belgium has made a great impact in the European Union, identifying itself not only as a great country, but also as a country filled with intelligent people. The culture of the different Belgian groups depicts which part of the country their group originates from. The culture, customs, and traditions of the people all differ. Belgium's cultural diversity has been enriched by both international and local immigration. The size of a country doesn't matter. It's the achievement that counts.

Belgium is cosmopolitan, urbanized, and densely inhabited. In the last one-hundred years, the Jews have been a growing immigrant community who comprise a sizable people group in Antwerp. As self employed business people, the Jews have given a face-lift to Antwerp's diamond tourist industry, managing jewel shops all over, beyond just the central station. The Chinese also run businesses throughout the country. Business relations between Belgium and China dated as far back as 1742, with countless ships from China sailing back and forth along the Scheldt River. Over the past decade, the Belgians have enjoyed successful business relations with China, which has contributed to sizable economic growth.

In my own experience I have enjoyed the good company of many Belgians. But, while many are friendly, many others are not. I've noticed that often in Belgium when you try to get closer to people, women in particular, they get scared, even though they may like you. They get upset when you try to get close to them but the moment you are unfriendly to them, they could end up hating you. At work, one of the ladies I have never greeted before for fear of angering her, constantly showed me a face of hatred until one day, when everything changed.

I saw her with her hands full of items and close to a door she couldn't open, so I quickly dashed to open the door for her. We exchanged names and since that day, we've been friends. There was one particular woman who always asked me if she had done anything wrong when I passed her without greeting her. There are others who do not want to see you, let alone greet you. Even though they can be very helpful to foreigners, often what they hate most is when the same foreigners solicit for fund or finance. Being African makes the matter worse because there seems to be a lack of trust. A black soliciting for fund to aid a project is not always successful because he can be seen as a con man, trying his con plan. It's a pity that some blacks are seen that way.

There are a lot of friendly Belgians. Some of them may even unexpectedly engage in conversation with you. This has happened many times. They make funny jokes too. Once I was waiting for the bus and it failed to come at the correct time. The Belgian I was waiting with tapped my shoulder and asked, "Do you know the reason buses in Antwerp are never punctual?" "I don't know," I answered. "Because the bus time schedules are written by women!" he said. I couldn't stop laughing.

When Belgians think they are wrong and being challenged, some will quickly threaten to call the police, because they may believe that the African challenging them is an illegal immigrant. But, when I put discrimination aside, I am really impressed by the way the Belgians prefer to keep their achievements to themselves. They are not noisy like the Dutch people. They are extremely intelligent people who are very humble. In their country, the police do not arrest anyone for smoking marijuana, yet the cities do not stink of it like some of the cities in the Netherlands do. The Belgians, including students, simply choose not to indulge in drugs. That is probably why there are fewer junkies in Belgium than there are in the Netherlands.

Like many people, the Belgians underestimate immigrants, especially Africans. I once went to a work agency of a Flemish community outside Antwerp called Heist op Den Berg, to register for some jobs. It was an hour journey from Antwerp and I desperately needed to use the restroom by the time I reached the office. I asked one of the female staff if I could use the toilet and she told me that the toilet was only for official use. For over ten minutes I searched for a place to relieve myself and couldn't hold it any longer. Eventually, I walked near a fence of an uncompleted building to ease myself. I feared someone calling the police but I escaped without intervention.

During the process of writing this book, I contacted three Belgians and asked them to write an essay about their people so that I could get actual facts from real Belgians. None were able to give me an account of their own people. One told me that the Belgians are strange people, but that was all she would say. Another referred me to a teacher I could contact on this subject, but the Flemish aren't as social as the Francophone. They love to be independent in everything and many times tried to do everything by themselves, which may seem selfish to some.

Many Africans have no desire to study when they arrive in Europe, because they've lived in poverty for so long. Ninety percent of them came for jobs and a better living while only ten percent came for learning and wealth. I would count myself to be among those who came to seek both wealth and education, since I didn't get the opportunity to seek much of the latter in Africa. When I arrived in Belgium a couple of years ago, I began studying the people, trying to learn who they really were. One doesn't need to do that with someone who comes from the Netherlands. You immediately know what kind of people they are by the way they talk, act, and comport themselves.

The Dutch are opposite of the Belgians though. They can be arrogant, noisy, abusers, and greedy and some have brought sickness, madness and other calamities to their own people, with what they call tolerance. Once, behind the Hotel Krasnapolsky in Amsterdam, I saw a young girl between the ages of fourteen and sixteen, smoking a big roll of marijuana. She looked dazed and confused so I asked her why she was doing this to herself. "Mind your own business," she told me. That is what the Dutch government has taught them to say to defend their country.

This is something I have not seen during my time in Belgium. The Belgians keep their children from engaging in such acts, which creates a healthy environment for their people. This is one of the ways I think Belgians exhibit intelligence. If you go to Amsterdam and explore the central train station to Bijlmer, a community lying in the South-East of Amsterdam, you can see how many people drugs have destroyed. Some of them look liked dead risen zombies, ready to act horror movies. But, in Antwerp and other Belgian cities, although drugs may have taken their toll on some of the people, it is not nearly as bad as it is in Holland because the Belgians discourage abusive drugs with campaigns. The Dutch, on the other hand, encourage it because the sales of drugs at their coffee shops sustain the tourism industry.

Instead of liberalism on soft drugs sustaining the economy in Antwerp, I witnessed many Cafés' dealings in drugs closed, actually helping prevent the boom of drug sales to citizens and teenagers.

The health care in Belgium is based on independent medical practice. Everyone has their own doctor for consultation. The patients pay the doctors and then get reimbursed by their insurance companies. Medicines are purchased at half-price with half paid by the insurance company.

One thing that disturbed me over and over again was the animosity between the Belgians. I noticed the relationship between the Flemish and the Walloons resembling the Palestinians and the Israelites relationship. Diplomatically though, they cope up as friendly neighbours. They don't attack each other with grenades, bombs, rockets and stones like the Israelites and the Palestinians. But, above all different political views have compounded them to continue living in non-violent hostility.

The country depends heavily on products that pass through the port in Antwerp. The port is accessible and one of the best and busiest seaports in the heart of Europe. It plays an active role in the global supply chain by sharing its knowledge and expertise with other ports worldwide. For ages, the port of Antwerp has served as an important platform for the European market with its good storage facilities offering marketing and other resources for many international shippers. It is estimated that in the year 2011, the port of Antwerp handled over eighty-five million tonnes of short-sea freight. This confirms that the port is the most important port in Europe.

In regards to the education system, Belgium enjoys high priority and quality education. It is therefore not a surprise to see the influx of immigrants pouring into Belgium schools to study with the high standard of their education. Both the French and the Flemish communities provide nursery, primary, middle or secondary schools, and the best universities, all available and readily accessible. In recent years, the academic institutions in all the three different language communities have developed a wide range of programmes and courses set in English, making it easy for international students and foreigners to enjoy their chosen careers.

There are journalism courses offered in English in some high institutions in Brussels, but none in Antwerp. Because of this, the immigrants from Francophone countries, including Africans, integrated easier when they settled in parts that spoke French. The immigrants from English speaking countries, however, had it very tough in Antwerp. This is the reason integration is poor in Flemish speaking provinces like Antwerp but not in the French-speaking communities.

After working and saving enough money to study journalism, I contacted a secretary working in the educational sector of Antwerp. Although she called many high institutions seeking my admittance, none of the high institution offered journalism in English in Antwerp. However in Antwerp in 2012, the Flemish association for investigative journalism held its tenth year anniversary at Plantijn College School. To mark the special anniversary, the programme's trainings and workshops were organised in English to attract a more international audience. Why, until then, had any high institution in the Flemish community of Antwerp failed to offer journalism in English as one of its courses? This is a problem that has forced many immigrants who are hungry to learn to abandon their passion and pursue a strange, unexpected career. This is the reason I became a forklift driver before I became a writer.

Among the Africans that immigrate to Belgium, there are doctors, engineers, pilots and other professionals. Unfortunately, because they often aren't officially recognized with certificates and diplomas, they have trouble integrating in Belgium. While I was busily writing this book, an article entitled "Foreign Doctors Ask For the Recognition of Their Diploma" appeared in the January 31, 2013 edition of the Flemish-written newspaper *De Standard* and it caught my attention. The story was about an African woman who is a doctor, fighting for the recognition of her certificates and diplomas as a medical doctor. "I have lost many years here," she said. She obtained her certificate in Tanzania as a medical assistant and in Russia as a medical doctor. She had already studied in Belgium for five years at the University of Antwerp and could speak Flemish fluently, but she is still schooling to get a job. According to her, Belgium makes it difficult for foreign doctors to practice their profession. This is true for more than just foreign doctors.

Like in many European countries, in Belgium, a foreigner can't just begin work with an outside school certificate which has created problems for immigrants integrating in Belgium. Even when it comes to race, there are places, especially Flemish communities like Antwerp, where immigrants are looked at differently. They are not socially prepared to accept those that look different from them.

Belgium once struggled with dealing with immigrants, particularly Africans. They can see them as economic intruders with a lack of an educational background. However, things have completely changed. In the past few years I have seen the best of everything, including the media, in Belgium. In 2002, to improve integration, a migration neutral law made it possible for immigrants to be naturalised linguistically, socially and economically.

One of the significant changes Belgian immigrants have seen recently is in sports. Many foreigners, including Africans, are in Belgium football playing for different clubs. One of these foreigners is Mbokani, a RSC Anderlecht player who won the "Golden Boot" after he was voted the best player in the Belgian league for his performances at home and Europe in 2012.

The Criss-cross Rhythm of Belgium's Politics and Their Future

One time when I was among other colleagues working on a compound, I silently listened to one of the heads of an institution warn a female colleague not to speak French.

"U moet niet spreken Frans hier," he said, which translated to "You must speak Netherlands here not French."

As an immigrant I am immensely passionate about knowing Belgium, its people, and its politics. This passion led me to the root of the problems between the Flemish and the Walloons. For instance, in the situation with the institution head and female colleague, it was unnecessary for the man to tell the woman to speak Dutch instead of French. After all, Belgium is one country with different languages. Therefore, whatever language is spoken should be respected and accepted at every office in the country.

This lack of unity between the Flemish and the Walloons has caused Belgium's political crisis. Even though they repeatedly struggle to find common ground between their people groups, life still goes on. Who could ever imagine that such a small country's politics could be so difficult? Why should a sect of people try to create and maintain barriers that would keep them divided?

Belgium's politics are much like former South African city, Apartheid's politics. The Flemish community is often unwilling to allow their own people to settle in the communities. Governing a country with politics based upon linguistic differences won't be successful. To prevent this, in the first week of January 2012, King Albert, deeply concerned about the fluctuations in Belgium's politics, warned political parties not to repeat the political climate of the 1930's. The King's comment evoked negative reactions from some of the political parties, including the Flemish nationalist party N-VA under Bart De Wever.

Premier Elio Di Rupo wasn't happy over the nationalist party's reaction to the King's comment and proceeded to call the N-VA party "a dangerous party for the country." Bart De Wever is not an easy politician to reckon with. He stepped in strongly with the slogan: "The Power For a Change" and was elected mayor of Antwerp. Ironically, the people who voted for him were the same people who hated him for his views and opinions. Everything Bart De Wever says is used against him, like when he asked some gay groups to avoid wearing t-shirts with inscriptions. Although you might think his opposition would enjoy this, making one devil in the name of politics is not a good idea for a nation. De Wever may have a good plan for his country, but his plans may not fit the nation. I know perfectly well that there is no way Belgium would thrive under 'separatism' type of government so it did not surprise me when the premier Elio Di Rupo called N-va a dangerous party.

The advocacy of separation from a group of people or a party can lead to rebellion. A leader of a country must see this, but still think and solve the problems of the people generally and not only for a specific group or people. If Bart De Wever continues to aspire to this form of governance, Belgium's politics will never know peace. Even though the nationalists are seeking nothing more than autonomy, critics see their quest as racial or ethnic segregation. The aim to establish this unpopular form of government in Western Europe bore ugly scars in Spain and Britain, as the Basque separatist movement, ETA, took arms against the Spanish government and the Irish Republican army against the British government. None succeeded and thousands of lives were lost.

In Belgium's lifespan, they have tasted the worst of criss-cross politics. Belgium's head of state, Yves Leterme could tell you this better than anyone else. Yves ruled Belgium twice, from March 20, 2008 to December 2008 and from November 2009 to Dec 6, 2011. After months of being unable to unite the Dutch and French speaking parties, Yves finally stepped out of the government arena and giving his letter of resignation to King Albert II which showed that since the political system is based on discussion and compromise, everything ends up in disarray when one party doesn't agree to something.

When I was a little boy in Africa, I often frequented the library. One of my favourite books was a book of the comic strip, *Tintin*. I never knew that the author of these great comic strips was Belgian, even after I noticed his name- Georges Rémi (Hergé). But when I arrived in the country, I finally made the connection. In every country, there is something that makes the region unique- it may be the tourist attractions, monuments, or great statutes, but sometimes it is about the products manufactured in the country, and Belgium is no exception. Belgium's beer and chocolate really makes it stand out. According to a newspaper I read recently, the country produces over one-thousand different kinds of quality beer and its quality chocolates are much appreciated throughout the whole world.

As the months advanced, I again noticed something else remarkable about the Belgians. Even though they are universally known for their great products, they keep a low profile and remain humble through all that they do. They know that "a good product doesn't need any advertising," so they relax and wait for customers to come to it, barely throwing any money into advertisements.

The Dutch fail to realise this. Instead they employ loud advertisements for their beer, making it known throughout the whole world.

The future of Belgium's politics, like someone stranded on the desert, has little hope for survival. There are clearly many storms yet to come. The only way Belgium may enjoy a stable political atmosphere in the future, is to create a state for all Belgians. They should eliminate linguistic barriers and political parties, burying their political differences, and unite as one people.

As Abraham Lincoln once said, "we here highly resolved that these dead shall not have died in vain, that this nation, under God, shall have a new birth of freedom; and that government of the people, by the people, for the people, shall not perish from the earth."

Accommodation and Advocacy Frauds

In the early stages of my stay in Belgium, I realised that many criminal activities were perpetrated by the indigenes in the accommodation sector and those in the advocacy service against foreigners looking for housing or resident permits. It was a time where it was practically impossible for a foreigner in Antwerp to find a clean house to rent. "Huisjesmelkers" or house milkers, are landlords who steal money from tenants, whether they are foreign or Belgian. Often, landlords would refuse to rent their houses to foreigners, especially Africans unless they were in deplorable condition. I inspected one of these houses at Borgerhout, a neighbourhood in Antwerp, and couldn't believe that such a terrible house was owned by a Belgian.

It was the most horrible house I had ever seen. With the state the house was in, it could have been a set for a horror movie. The building wasn't completed and everything in the house looked like the aftermath of an earthquake. There was even a toilet in the kitchen. I don't know what kind of architect would design such a house. I asked the woman how a toilet could be in a small kitchen like that.

She responded, "there was a window to open." When I turned to leave, she hurled after me, "If you don't like it, someone else will."

I believed her because any desperate African, who really had no place to lay his head, wouldn't object to renting that place, regardless of the health hazards.

I contacted a Belgian woman I knew to see if she could help me find a house. She called the owner of a house and told her that she was trying to help a worker who couldn't get a house. The owner of the house asked her where I came from and when she told her that I was an African, she told her that she doesn't rent her house to Africans. When the Belgian woman asked her the reason, the homeowner said it was because Africans do not keep their houses clean.

When my friend asked the owner of the house if "she had ever seen a real dirty white man before," she couldn't answer and hung up the phone.

Finally, after searching for a good place to rent, I found a single bedroom apartment near Antwerp's central station. Because house hunting caused me to lose my interest in living in Antwerp, I signed a contract to live only four months at the place. I told the landlord that four months would be enough for me to look for another place outside Antwerp and he agreed, as long as I paid for a three month gurantee. This is known in the Flemish community as "waarborg" or advance payment or guarantee. The purpose of paying three months guarantee was to keep the place in good shape and avoid damage and he wanted that money in cash. He informed me that he was not interested in renting me a room paid by the social service, O.C.M.W.

He had a reason for this. Social services would not hand him such an amount of cash. They would need to deposit it at the bank and the documents would be prepared by both parties. Many landlords don't like this system, but the majority of those who hate that payment system are simply fraudsters with a mind to cheat their tenants. That was the kind of landlord who rented his house to me. The apartment was cockroach-infested and living there in for just a week was a nightmare. Cockroaches crawled on me every night and they were all over the house. They fed on my bread and many on my cooked food. Tenants who couldn't handle the situation quickly abandoned the property, leaving and losing their three months guarantee. It's because of situations like this that landlords request a cash guarantee.

My dishonest landlord was aware of this problem. This was why he rented his house to foreigners who weren't assisted by the social service. He brought me an insecticide to use to kill the cockroaches, but even that couldn't help. A Nepalese couple lived on the third floor. When his pregnant wife could no longer climbed the stairs, he gave our landlord the required three months notice, yet when he was ready to leave, the landlord refused to give him his guarantee of 27,000 Belgian francs (which amounts to nearly 669 Euros). Likewise, when I gave notice, despite his full knowledge of my short term lease, he took 9,000 Belgium francs from the 27,000 Belgium francs I had given to him.

I confronted him with the real reason he doesn't want to rent a house to anyone assisted by the social service. His designed scheme was to steal money from foreigners. I demanded my money back and warned him that if he did not refund my money, I would not make it easy for him. He thought that statement was an empty boast. He thought he had a reason to underestimate me. He was a Belgian and Belgians often don't see foreigners, especially Africans, as a threat. No one really cares about them and everyone treats them with impunity. But I would not be underestimated. I decided to let the mayor of Antwerp, a lady called Leona Detigé, know about this problem.

I first published the story in *The Voice* magazine, an African magazine published in the Netherlands. I supported the story with pictures and the name of my landlord. I also sent a letter, attached to the copy of the publication, to the mayor. She took swift action, quickly responding because her administration had been trying finding ways to prevent nefarious activities like these from going on in the city. The mayor forwarded the letter and the published story to the head of the police department at Handel Street. I was at work one day when I received a call from the police asking about the case.

Before my appointment, I was able to trace three other people whom the landlord had stolen money from. I tried to convince them to join me to the police station as fellow fraud victims, but they refused. They did not want to get involved with the police. Two of them feared that investigations by the police would affect their quest for resident permit. That is the fear of most Africans in Europe. Many take advantage of this and commit crimes against Africans, because as illegal immigrants they fear the police. Out of the three people I approached, only the Nepalese man agreed to tell his story to the police. The two defrauded Africans refused.

I spoke at length to the police officer and proved that the landlord was a criminal preying on foreigners. After about twenty-five minutes of interrogation, another policeman in plainclothes came in. When he learned the reason we had come, he retorted mockingly, "If we knew the landlord was like that, why did you rent the house?" That was the end of the case as far as the police were concerned. Since the police didn't take any action, I knew the fraud would persist with his schemes, so I chose to take the law into my own hands in a non-violent but innovative way. Tenants kept moving in because he had written on the house "Te Huur" which means " to rent."

I boldly printed posters that read "Don't be a victim. The owner of this house is a criminal who steals the 'waarborg' of foreigners. Be wise and keep away from this house," in English and Netherlands and pasted it all over the houses' windows and doors. Before going to work in the morning, I passed around the house to see if the posters were still there. Some of them had been removed, so I pasted new ones up. I did this same inspection after work as well. Once, I was putting fresh posters on the windows, when I spotted a police van behind me. The two policemen in the van stopped to read what I was pasting on the windows and without a question they moved away.

Another time, I was coming to see if the posters were on the windows, when I caught the landlord removing the posters from the windows. As I hastily headed to meet him, he abandoned his car and fled towards the central train station, scared. I don't know how old he was, but he was the fastest runner I had ever seen and he escaped after I gave him a very hot chase. I came back to where he had parked his car and deflated one of his car tyres to prevent him from escaping. I wanted my money and I would have done anything to get it back. I waited for him for over two hours but he never came back. I then left and headed home. In the morning when I came, the car was gone.

I continued to post the warnings on the windows and doors for three months. This hurt his business so badly that no one rented the house for a long time. But this was not the end of the story. Eventually, I rented a house on the outskirts of Antwerp. The vindictive landlord was able to trace me to my new place and report me to the police. They brought me into their office for questioning. The police on duty read my charges to me and asked if I understood the contents of the letter. "It's a serious crime," he said. I told the officer that the police department at Handel Street knew about the case and was in charge of the investigation. He asked for proof of my claim, but I didn't have it with me so he asked me to go home and bring it. When I finally presented them to him, he was satisfied and sent me home.

When the police in Borsbeek, where my new place was located, contacted the man and informed him that they couldn't charge me for any offence since the Handel Street police department were handling the case, he was so disappointed that he went mad. He sent the case to court. In the letter of summons to appear in court, his lawyer stated that I wasn't living in the house any longer, but I continued to post things on his apartment windows and doors Which had prevented people from renting the house and cost him revenue. His client filed for compensation of almost three hundred Euros. I refused to appear in court and instead sent a registered letter attached to the police report of the case. I asked the lawyer to judge who really should be compensated in this situation and I didn't hear from any of them again.

Other foreigners, particularly Africans were defrauded daily in Antwerp by lawyers as well. I remember a lawyer who collected one thousand Euros from my friend David with the promise of helping him gain nationality and a Belgian passport. This was a fraud, because he hadn't even had a valid white card for a year yet. A foreigner could only apply for Belgian nationality if he had lived in Belgium for at least five to seven years. He must be in possession of a white card, as evidence by his registered name in the foreign register. Despite all of this, there were some genuine lawyers serving foreigners in honesty.

If I've learned anything, it's that criminality is universal, but being black seems to bring more unwarranted suspicion. In Antwerp, a lawyer collected over six hundred Euros from her African client with the promise of doing everything on his behalf to get him his documents, since he'd been in the country for ten years. She failed her client and angered the man. Even though he didn't threaten her, she proceeded to call the police and tell them that her client paid her with fake Euro currency. Interestingly enough, she couldn't seem to provide proof of this "fake currency."

I started seeing the best part of Belgium's judiciary system when Annemie Turtelboom was appointed the Minister of Justice in Elio Di Rupo's government. As member of the Open Flemish Liberals and Democrats and as an experienced politician, Annemie was the minster of migration and asylum policy in Leterme's government before she became the minister of interior in Van Rompuy's government on July 17, 2009. There were rampant frauds reported by many advocates who were representing foreigners. I often heard reports of people duped by their lawyers, but you rarely read anything about that in the newspapers.

I know that Annemie knew about this problem before she assumed the post of Minister of Justice. Her inception has overhauled the judiciary system completely. Annemie Tutelboom committed to changing many things, including the law on arbitration, in the course of her term of office. True justice brings the best satisfaction for victims of diverse unpleasant situations. That is the commitment of the justice minister. In August 2012, after meeting protest for the early release of the Belgian paedophile and killer Marc Dutroux, the justice minister met the parents of the girls he killed and gave them assurance by informing them of changes in the judicial system to give victims more rights and a stronger voice.

The African's Inhumanity to the African

In all fairness, some black people have been responsible for the indifference shown by the police service to black communities. It takes many years to build a good reputation and it takes only a fraction of a second for a fool to destroy years of good work. Some Africans in Europe have sold themselves to the police. Stories of crime, drugs, and prostitution come to the desk of the police everyday. There are informants within the black community and because of this there are few secrets that the police don't know about the African community. One time at the Borgerhout district police station in Antwerp, a police officer asked me why Africans liked reporting themselves to the police so often and I couldn't answer. So I just smiled.

I heard a story of a 22-year old African prostitute working for a prominent woman who was known as a god-mother, bringing young African girls into Belgium to work as prostitutes. Like all the others, the girl was deceived into thinking that she was coming to work for a madam in a European business for two years to pay the woman a $60,000 debt. In reality, her job was to sell her body to pay up this debt. By the time she discovered that she had been deceived, she had no choice but to engage in full prostitution to pay her debt. Sadly, she didn't make enough money to repay her debt within that stipulated period and the woman hired other pimps to teach her a lesson.

These pimps overpowered her, tying her down and burning her with a red-hot pressing iron. Then they parted her legs and sprayed hot pepper into her vagina, leaving her to bleed to death. She managed to call some of her friends who rushed her to the hospital. She spent seven months trying to recover, but her injuries were so extensive that she died. On May 23, 2001, she was buried at the Merksem cemetery in Antwerp. I had heard of the cruelty between Africans before, but these cruelties exceeded all I had heard of in Antwerp. In fact, this woman is not only one to fall victim to the organised crime of human trafficking.

In April, 2006, another Nigerian prostitute was asked by her doctor to rest, which angered her pimp because she couldn't work for two days. She was then pushed down the staircase of a storey building by her pimp and died of her injuries. The Antwerp police department and the mayor took swift action to hunt down the pimps throughout the city. A week long police campaign to cripple the prostitution and drug trade led to the rounded up of over 60 African prostitutes, mainly from Nigeria and Ghana. They were then deported to their respective countries. Police investigations revealed that some of the deported prostitutes had previously been deported from Germany and Italy, and somehow found their way back into the country. The police closed down part of the red light district.

The few streets that were booming with prostitution in Antwerp closed down. In fact, every measure that could possibly hamper the activities of prostitution was taken. Many pimps and prostitutes were arrested and the prostitution trade fell. A police vehicle was stationed at "Connicksplein," a notorious neighbourhood in Antwerp, known for illegal activities like drug trafficking and prostitution, to assess the situation. With prostitution trade in disarray and no illegal money for the pimps, a group calling itself the "Nigerian Mafia" sent a warning letter to the police threatening them that they were ready to fight them to death for driving their women off streets. I wrote about the story in *The Voice* magazine and sent copies to the police. To develop and beautify the area after getting rid of all the nefarious activities, the city built a modern library. Connicksplein is now a safe place to walk even in the night. It used to be a very dangerous place.

The Sierra Leone Welfare Association in Antwerp, (SLAWA) once lost one of its members there. After the war in Sierra Leone, indigenes from the country who made it to Europe, formed the Sierra Leone association to cater to the needs of their citizens. It is one of the only survived African associations in Antwerp. Once, a SLAWA member saw two people fighting and he went to separate them like a good Samaritan. He was then stabbed in the neck for trying to help and died at a hospital in Antwerp, with tears running down his face.

If Africans are cruel to each another in these ways and show little love or sympathy to their fellow man, how do they expect to gain society's to love or respect? Africans need to set a good example and lead clean lives in society. This could bring back the respect we crave. Investigations of these situations over time have revealed many disturbing results. On many occasions, children brought to Belgium by adults are forced into prostitution and threatened with violence or death if they refuse. I published a story similar to this and when those involved got a copy of the magazine, they sought to deal with me, but since I know that what I do is risky, nobody knows where I live. That saved me.

In another shocking situation, I covered a story sometime ago about a woman who forced her daughter into prostitution to recoup the money she spent to bring her to Europe. When the girl refused to comply, there was a big row between the daughter and mother. In my previous published book "Overseas Chronicle," I emphasized what Africans do against their fellow Africans in Holland, particularly Amsterdam. They dominate and act as informants toward their own African brothers and sisters.

In Amsterdam, I witnessed the prayers of one African woman against her fellow African, wishing her to be an illegal immigrant for the rest of her life. How could one offer such prayers to God? This is only the tip of the iceberg. The Amsterdam police could tell you more. In general, Africans there are seen as brutal, savage, merciless, senseless, and undesirable. Unfortunately, this negative perception has affected and overshadowed any intelligent ones. They are never seen. Mothers waged war against their own children, taxing them and extracting money from them for the cost of bringing them from Africa to Europe.

Most of the children who can't handle these situations simply go to the police station to lodge complaints against their parents and relatives. A young girl, about eighteen years old, told the police that "the person who brought me into this country is not my real mother. She has forced me into prostitution." The police have confirmed some of these reports that come to me. Unbelievably, sums of money ranging from $50,000 to $60,000 are taken from the victims of human trafficking.

Some are forced to swear an oath that if they are not able to pay the amount that they owe, which often causes them to go mad or die. With this kind of threat, the scared and tormented girls are forced to sleep with as many men as their bodies can take. The results are always disastrous. The rebirth of modern slavery involving blacks against fellow blacks is totally inhuman.

Education is very poor in Africa because of all the expenses involved. Many children and adults aren't able to have proper education there which has caused more poverty in impoverished Africa. It felt like a dream to me when I landed at the European shore, because my pursuit was higher education. Even when I couldn't further my career in journalism, I still gave thanks to the many people who partially and wholly helped me gain knowledge in Europe, that I lacked in Africa. I had my first computer and technological knowledge in Belgium. I appreciate and love the Belgians for helping me in many things regardless of the few emotional setbacks.

Because of this, I am expecting other Africans to learn too. Unfortunately, at times the way some Africans in Belgium behave ignorantly makes me feel ashamed. Since many lack education, they also lack manners. In the public transport, you can often hear an African speaking on the phone all the way across the bus or train.

The Political Crimes of Belgium in Africa

In 1914, when the Germans invaded Belgium during the war, they committed many grievous atrocities against the civilian population. It is estimated that nearly 6,000 Belgians were killed and 25,000 homes and 837 communities were also destroyed. This historical fact is known by some as the greatest crime against Belgium in their history. To a peace-loving country like Belgium, the period of destruction was tough for them to handle. Although, compared to what King Leopold II did to Congo during the colonial era, one can see that what the Germans did to the Belgians was just the tip of the iceberg. Nevertheless; crime, whether big or small, should be punished, even though many seem to elude it.

The swift European scramble over African territory took place from the 17th century to the 20th century. The European kingdoms, including France, England and Belgium, took advantage of the cordial friendship and trust between them and the tribal chiefs and plundered the continent. Amongst the greediest and brutal colonisers was King Leopold II of Belgium. Leopold colonised Congo, which officially became his personal property in 1876. The world witnessed the slaughter in Congo under Leopold's reign and criticisms came from every angle.

In 1884 during the Berlin Conference, Leopold pledged to discourage the ongoing East African slave trade, promote humanitarian policies, and guarantee a twenty-year free trade within the colony. But contrary to all the pledges he made in the 1880's, he issued the decrees in his favour, therefore violating the conditions he pledged at the Berlin Conference. His decrees monopolized all of their resources, forcing the natives to deliver every found ivory and tapped rubber to state officers. Many men were mercilessly exploited and some were driven to death. To ensure his demand would be satisfied, Leopold's men held the wives and the children of the rubber tappers hostage until they brought him exactly what he wanted.

Those unable to supply his demand often had their villages burned down, their children murdered, or their hands cut off. King Leopold of Belgium was the first person to implement this kind of cruelty towards children, before the brutal civil war in Sierra Leone that claimed thousands of lives. As I researched further, I saw photographs of children with hacked wrists and limbs. The chiefs, even though they fought back against Leopold's men, were quickly defeated and many fled to hide in the bush. Leopold sent his men to chase after them in the forest, giving them instructions to bring the right hand of every killed victim as a proof.

To satisfy their greed and resources without confrontation, the Europeans hatched a plan to cause tribal conflicts throughout Africa. Germans lost interest in Rwanda after the First World War and the Belgians took over. The Belgians ruled Rwanda through the Tutsi, using them at their disposal. The Tutsis', who were mainly cattle keepers, herds grew at a very rapid pace. They grew so rapidly, that the Hutus, who were farmers, had no more land to accommodate the Tutsis' animals. The Belgians could have prevented this land issue from turning into bloodshed, but they ignored the problem and a great massacre began. Streams of blood flowed in Rwanda. The peasants burned down households and cut throats, and this all occurred under the nose of the Belgian media, who did nothing to prevent it.

The Tutsis, an educated and ambitious tribe, demanded their freedom, which was something the Belgians were utterly unprepared to handle. Instead of giving in to the demand of the educated Tutsis, the Belgians did something unthinkable: they switched tactics by abandoning the Tutsis and supporting the more submissive Hutus instead. They begin to incite them against the Tutsis. The Belgians were successful in their attempts and the Hutus took up arms against the Tutsis.

The freshest part of Rwanda's bloodshed ignited after the death of a Hutu and the president, Juvenal Habyarimana, when his plane was shot down in Kigali in April 1994. Ethnic violence in Rwanda is nothing new. But as a country once under Belgium, many expect the Belgium government and media to play an important role in solving ethnic conflicts like these. Africa always seems to neglect solving conflicts of this nature until last minute when the situation gets worse, right before help finally comes in. The piles of human skulls in Rwanda after the war resembled those from the killing fields of Cambodia. It is estimated that nearly 800,000 people were massacred in the genocide.

Belgium was among those powers that the African independence movement caught by surprise after the arrival of Dr. Kwame Nkrumah in Ghana, from United States of America. Ghana became the first country to attain independence in the sub-Saharan Africa under the influence of Dr. Kwame Nkrumah. He declared **"The independence of Ghana is meaningless, unless it is linked up with the total liberation of Africa".**

This was a clear warning message to the colonial leaders that he was going to fight to liberate every African country under colonial rule.

Kwame Nkrumah's warning wasn't an empty boast. He quickly started his campaign against the colonial masters. He helped his friend Ahmed Sekou Touré of the Republic of Guinea break free from France in 1958. France was so disappointed and angry that they took everything from the state house in Conakry, including the furniture, back to

France. Sekou Touré wouldn't tolerate sitting on the floor. He furnished the state house. They pulled their support from France, who in turn planned more difficulties for Sekou Touré's administration.

Nkrumah was a pillar force and stumbling block against colonial masters. They planned his assassination by causing disturbances in Ghana and other parts of Africa. Then, what the Belgians feared most and prayed wouldn't happen occurred. They lost their grip on Congo. Nkrumah joined hands with his friend Patrice Lumumba and they fought the Belgians squarely, finally liberating the country in June 1960. This was the biggest blow the Belgians have endured to this day. They are still recovering from the impact of losing their grip on Congo today. The bitterness in their hearts is deep and could take many years to heal.

"A day will come when history will speak. Africa will write down its own history. It will be a history of glory and dignity," declared Patrice Lumumba, as the first premier of Congo.

To gain revenge after losing their colony, the Belgians planned the assassination of Patrice Lumumba. His association with Kwame Nkrumah and successful liberation of Congo prompted the CIA and the Belgians to plan the assassination of two great African leaders. Just six months after assuming power, Lumumba was toppled in a military coup. He was killed by firing squad commanded by a Belgian officer. His best friend Nkrumah was also toppled in a military coup, supported by the CIA in 1966. He lived in exile in Conakry-Guinea and died in Bucharest, Romania under treatment.

I've asked myself many times if Europeans and Americans know or think about the damage, destruction, and carnage they've inflicted on Africa. Some say it has to happen in order to fulfil history while others say that it's a crime that's been committed with impunity. Whatever the case may be, Africans have awakened from their slumber. They are all over Europe now, trying to enjoy what some men have taken from them. The mass emigration to Europe can only be stopped if Europe and America invest in Africa, creating more work, schools and health facilities. Since it hasn't been done yet, emigration cannot be stopped or controlled.

Even though the Belgians have apologised for all the carnage and suffering they caused in Africa during the colonial era, including the assassination of Patrice Lumumba, their apology can't heal the wounds of the victim's relatives. The blood stain of those they murdered will always remain on their unwashed palms. As a punishment to Ghana after Nkrumah's interference in Congo's politics, the Belgian government has vowed to never build their embassy in Ghana. Even though this hasn't been openly said or officially written anywhere in a book, one doesn't need to be intelligent to know this. Ghana is a great country that deserves a Belgian Embassy, not a Consulate.

The media plays an important role in informing and protecting society. History reveals that the media in Belgium has made some mistakes in the past. When I joined the Flemish Journalists Association a couple of years ago, I thought that by now the Belgian media had learned a lesson from their past mistakes. The media was very strong on issues like political debate, economic exchange, entertainment and recreation but weak when it came to issues like community building and solving racial problems. The latter is the reason that creating a stable government became the biggest problem in the country. There was even a time when Belgium was without a leader for 535 days, due to political crisis.

Racism is a universal problem. It's a problem that cannot be eliminated, but it can be reduced. Everyone has dealt with it; politicians, churches, spiritual leaders and community activities are all a part of solving the problem, even though some of the problems continue. People are not born racists. It's society that influences people to hate others because of the colour of their skin. The concept of skin colour superiority was born long ago and everyone has witnessed the misery and carnage racism has caused in our society. To create a better society and build a stable community, we have to expect the best from the media, even when they don't always pull through.

The media in Belgium, especially in Antwerp, was among the failed media systems that couldn't seem to help solve racial issues. In the early part of the year 2000, I wasn't pleased in the performance of the media in regard to foreigners. It seemed to me that they created more enmity for foreigners than anything else. They didn't play a role in better integration. Surprisingly, now I can classify Belgium's media as one of the best in Europe. They have realised their mistakes and made an excellent and swift transformation. Sometimes I wonder how they were able to achieve this. One thing society fears most is exposure by the opposition, which doesn't do good things. Which one is better, to speak out and be an enemy or be loved by everyone, because you don't care about truth?

"I bought a gun to kill people of foreign origin, but the death of the Belgian child is a mistake." These were the words of the racist killer as he lay on his hospital bed at the Stuivenberg hospital on May 13, 2006, that sent shock waves throughout Antwerp. The 18-year-old student of Vrij Agroen Biotechnisch Institute (VABI) in Roeselare, admitted this during his interview with the media. Unfortunately, the gun didn't only take the life of the African woman from the Republic of Mali, but also that of the small innocent Belgian child that the deceased was baby-sitting.

The killer's 500 Euros hunter's gun also hit a Turkish woman reading nearby, but she survived. Many wonder why such dramatic things take place in Antwerp when it's such a small city. This was a time in Antwerp's history where the media wasn't doing enough to protect foreigners, particularly Africans. Then, racism was stronger than a hurricane. When this was taking place, I wrote "a crooked plant can be straightened when it is still young and growing. You can't straighten it up, after it has fully grown. In this case the problem of racism should have been tackled from its roots, but not from the stem or branches. I appreciate all the efforts many organisations in Antwerp and Brussels are making, against racism. Unfortunately, this fight would amount to nothing, because the tree of racism has already grown and matured in the city of Antwerp."

I further stressed that "if organisations want a change then they should follow a different course to let racial offenders pay heavily for their crime, possible a jail sentence, especially in Antwerp, where racial offenders break the law with impunity."

The relationship between the indigenes of Antwerp with the foreigners at that time was very poor. I wrote about this problem and sent copies of the publication to the police stations around Antwerp. I am not a Messiah or a saviour, destined to save mankind. But I try my best, in a non-violent way, to use *The Voice* magazine to alert the police about what was goes wrong in society. This worked for me then and as time advanced, I saw changes gradually take place for Africans in Antwerp.

Public Enemy Number One

Sometimes I think that I might enjoy Belgium more if I were to walk around aimlessly smoking marijuana and sitting outside, joining other Africans drinking beer at tables along the streets each summer. I might also enjoy my life fully if I were totally ignorant and without a conscious mind to notice what the wrongdoings towards foreigners, including Africans. God only knows how many times I have wept in my prayers to see my fellow Africans doing something better in the Antwerp community and how many times I've lost sleep just dreaming about the African community in Antwerp aspiring to greater things in life so that I can wear a smile on my face.

In Antwerp, many African associations formed as a platform to enhance and support illegal immigrants and fellow Africans who were finding problems with integrating into Belgium. Most of these associations have since collapsed. There was a particular one which was registered and known by the Antwerp province and police. The members of this association who paid their membership fee were issued membership cards. The association was widely accepted and gained a good name, which allowed any controlled illegal immigrant to be set free when they showed their membership card. Unfortunately though, the chairman who had access to the financial account of the association started using the membership fees himself, until there was no longer any funds in the association's coffers to pay the offices they had rented and the association collapsed.

Upon finding that out, I stepped in strongly, trying my best and supporting the association monthly with 150 Euros of my hard earned money. Despite my efforts, it collapsed. The former association office is now serving as an African market. Later, another association was formed because of the bitter experience we had when the first one collapsed. We were very lucky that one of the African women, married to a Belgian, could provide us with office equipment, including photocopy machines and computers. We learned that even when you have a group of good people, there can be a hypocrite in disguise. Without our knowledge, one of our own head officers made a compilation list and applied for subsidy from the City of Antwerp. But, when the truth came out and he was confronted, he abandoned the association with shame and it collapsed.

Sometimes I ask myself if it worth to help Africans at all if they aren't ready to sacrifice to achieve better lives in the European communities. I have received many complaints from those who lost their loved ones at a hospital called

'Stuivenberg' in Antwerp. There are many hospitals in Antwerp, but the death rate of Africans in this particular hospital was greater than any other hospital in Antwerp. According to the Africans, they thought something was amiss at the hospital and suspected that the doctors at the hospital killed patients and stole the body organs of Africans when the Belgians desperately needed organs.

The need for organ donors is increasing worldwide and regrettably many people are unwilling to donate an organ to save the life of a person. As the gap between the supply and demand for organ donors continued to widen, in Antwerp, some organizations distributed letters to encourage donors. This is why I answered the call of the Africans to investigate this situation. According to some of their reports, a patient could be there with a leg injury or other non-lethal problem, but die in strange circumstances anyways. It wasn't my wish to do this investigation for a name for myself. I did it because a few Africans approached me for help investigating. Prior to this investigation, I had witnessed a demonstration by a group of Albanians at the hospital over similar accusations.

The fear of losing loved ones at the Stuivenberg Hospital hung on the heads of foreigners, especially Africans, so the mere mention of the hospital's name made many tremble with fear. On May 3, 2006, I visited the hospital to start my investigations. Being a Black man made the matter worst because often we are overshadowed by underestimation. I might have been received differently if I were a Belgian journalist. I was directed to more than four different places which frustrated me into nearly abandoning my cause until finally, I met the secretary. She refused to tell me her name, even when I showed her my Belgian press card, as a member of Flemish Journalists Association.

According to her, the hospital had existed for over one-hundred years, so if such a malpractice was occurring, the government would have closed it down immediately. I debunked this by commenting that since this was against foreigners, no newspaper would dare expose them. Of what newspaper will expose the doctors in Belgium if they knew such things were going on? You often read about petty crimes committed by foreigners in Antwerp, but what the Belgians do against foreigners does not appear anywhere in their newspapers. The secretary drove me away from her office. Her attitude towards me was shocking.

"Your behaviour and your refusal to allow me to do my investigation is enough to believe that the Stuivenberg Hospital is indeed killing foreigners to steal their body parts," I told her as I parted. I published the investigation and sent copies of the magazine to the police stations at Berchem, Oudaan, Handel Street, a branch of an integration office affiliated with the city of Antwerp and the

Ministry of Interior Affairs in Brussels. After this everything seemed to go back to normal, until my wife told me that an officer from the Berchem police department called to see me when I wasn't home and left a note for me to call on him at the station.

I did and the officer spoke nicely to me about the publication, believing that nothing of that sort was going on. I was then called by the integration office for a meeting, scheduled at 20.00 PM, which I thought was too late for a meeting. Because of that, I declined attending the meeting.

Three years went by and I was raising funds for the publication of one of my books. I called on a woman working at the Integration Department of the City of Antwerp. I went to the wrong place at the wrong time in regard to my previous publications. After giving her a little insight to the project I was handling, I asked if the department could give me any help.

I was shocked by her sudden attack. "If it's because of your books that you came to me, I can't offer you any help". She went on to talk about the publication of the investigation at the Stuivenberg hospital, asking me of what kind of journalist I was to publish such a stupid story. Stupid Story? It seems that whatever the Blackman writes against whites is often disregarded. Not this time. The world is rapidly changing. We have gone through many degrading, painful experiences and now that the chains are broken, the black man has democratic freedom and the right to express his own opinions and rights.

She said that her husband was a journalist and would never publish a baseless story like that, even though her husband had published several baseless articles on AIDS in Africa. She has forgotten that homosexuality originated in Europe before it gradually spread to Africa. The Acquired Immune Deficiency Syndrome (AIDS) is currently equally killing Europeans and Africans, yet it has been written that the sickness originated in Africa. Africans didn't call that publication stupid or baseless. We accepted it, simply knowing it's not true.

"Just look, the story is full of mistakes," she remarked. She went on to question my integrity as a qualified journalist. I waited for her to do all the talking and after she completed whatever she had to say, I said to her "I don't feel any remorse for publishing this article. There is a always a little truth in rumours. I published this article at the instance of the people of the African community. Your husband is a journalist, but he is Belgian, not African. Secondly, you were complaining about the mistakes in the article to discredit me as far my profession is concerned. If you spoke good English, you could see that the publication begins with "Our correspondent investigations at the Stuivenberg Hospital". This means that I presented my report to someone and the person is writing on my behalf. Therefore the mistakes don't come from me".

I went on to tell her that if she wanted to read the introduction of the script to my first book and point out any mistake she came across. She took and started to read. As she read, she reached the part where I remark about my Belgian press card and she queried, "What? What? What? Do you have a press card here?" I showed it to her. She examined it and lamely said, "It is not the same as the one my husband has." She should have accepted my claim without reading, but she got it when she read some of my book. Her underestimation of me here was heavier than a metal iron. It is rare to see a black journalist in Belgium, and up until recently, I hadn't seen any black journalist serving in print or electronic media anywhere around here. Only time will tell.

The woman was surprised to read that I had a press card because she hadn't heard of any black men in Belgium achieving it. However, I didn't buy the card. I applied for membership and after the committee were satisfied with my requirements as a professional journalist, they accepted me as a member. According to her, after my publication, they sent a delegation to all the hospitals in Antwerp to investigate. Whether it is true or not, her actions toward me further prove my claim that there is discrimination in Antwerp, just like there is anywhere else.

I don't hate any Belgian. I have met honest ones who have helped me more than what any African had done for me. As I stayed longer in the country, I became more familiar with them and tried to understand them. Every country has an immigration problem. It has been the priority of every government, especially in Western Europe, to fight against the influx of immigrants which makes it total chaos for the citizens when unemployment sours. Most of these immigrants indulge in various crimes and many hang on tax payers hard earned money as benefit. This is exactly what Belgium, like any other European country, fears. Many times, foreigners who seem to not to understand these curtailing measures usually say the people of this country are racists. That doesn't mean that there is no racism in Belgium. Racism is a universal problem.

Once when writing for the Voice Magazine, I got information from a certain female project coordinator about a black police chief in the community in which she lived and she asked if I was interested in interviewing him, offering to do the arrangements for me. "A black police boss in Belgium?," I asked."Yes," she said. I had seen hundreds of black bus drivers, police officers, civil servants holding high positions in other countries and I saw similar things in Holland too since they colonised a few black countries, including Surinam, but Antwerp was different. You can see blacks in Antwerp every day, but it would take you years to see a black man in police uniform, just like it took me five years to encounter the first black bus driver in the city.

The arrangement was made and I met the police chief called Eddie Battle. The nice looking gentleman sat behind his desk and started telling me his story about being a black child growing up in a purely white environment. "Could you imagine being the only black child in your school from elementary school throughout to high school? Could you imagine being the only black in almost every setting, including your own home? Well believe it or not, I have experienced both of those things." According to him, he was born in a small village called Boom, near Antwerp on March 30, 1946. His father was a black American soldier who was stationed in Europe at the end of Second World War and his mother a native from Belgium.

As a teenager he went to live with his grandparents. Even though he encountered racism on daily basis, he said he never discussed his problems with his grandparents. "They never knew I was being discriminated against," he said. Because he was the only black child in the school and totally different from his other school mates, he experienced many unpleasant situations, but chose to never become aggressive. Instead, he chose to always be quiet. Because of his quiet nature and calmness, his schoolmates and teachers thought he was dumb. He recalled one of his teachers who teaches Algebra in his junior high school asking him “to stand at the corner of the classroom everyday for no reason.” Faced with that kind of pressure on daily basis, he became introverted with strong “will” and determination to make it in life. “In a way, it was good for me because I hard to work hard to prove that I am not dumb but capable and knowledgeable,” said Mr. Battle.

He said that after high school, he joined the army for 15 months. After the serving in the army, he tried to find a job but because of the colour of his skin, he couldn't find one. His grandfather then told him to apply to join the police department. He took the entrance examination which was of two parts: the theory and the practical sections. He passed the theory examination, a written test, but because of discrimination he told me that he “failed the verbal part of the examination”. Mr. Eddie Battle knew that the hotter the battle, the sweeter the victory. Because of this, he didn't give up. He was encouraged to take the test again and he did. Out of the 65 pupils who entered the Police Academy, he finished number one.

Despite all the racial problems he encountered, he excelled at the Police Academy and has risen through the ranks to the top of his craft. While working at the police department, he attended the university of Brussels where he gained a Masters degree in criminology and education. He reached the top of his career with promotions. In the year 2001, he was appointed the police chief. His fame and success attracted the media to his office many times. He has been interviewed several times for national television, newspapers and magazines. He has been happily married for 44 years and has a beautiful daughter who is 42.

Finally, before I left his office, Mr. Battle gave me words of wisdom- some valuable advice which has been my guide till now. "If you work hard and believe in yourself, you can become whatever you want to be. Don't think too much about discrimination but instead think about what you want to become in life". On this note, I thanked him for his time and what I had learned from him. I learned to never put myself down even if they try hard to put me down. I hope this can be a lesson for all of us. This racism concept must be defended. There is racism in every race.

Who is a racist, after all? Let's begin in Africa. There have been a couple times that I have seen parents angry with their daughters for marrying a man from another clan. In Ghana, people talk negative things about the Ewes, a tribe from the Volta region of Ghana. An Ashanti doesn't like a Ga, from the Greater Accra Region. In Nigeria the Igbo hates the Yoruba. In Sierra Leone, the Creole doesn't like the Susu or Mende. In Rwanda, hatred between the Hutus and Tutsis, led to the genocide. Islam speaks about togetherness and love for all mankind, yet in Iraq, Saddam Hussein was killing his own people who weren't from his tribe.

Now we are in Europe, where civil war erupted in Bosnia, because of ethnic conflict. The persecution in Eastern Europe against Jews, Gypsies and other foreigners was one of the biggest crimes committed against mankind. And Belgium falls apart when the Flemish and Walloons don't find common goals. A member of parliament once said that "we don't want them to come to live in our territory to ruin our culture," when remarking on the Walloons. This is not a statement of discrimination, but pure racism. There is racism in everyone.

This statement also supports my claim that integration in Antwerp is very poor. If the Flemish don't want their own people, the Walloons, to settle with them, how could they allow foreigners to settle with them either? Every country, especially small ones like Belgium, tries to protect its citizens and borders against illegal immigrants, but the way they handle things concerning foreigners is sometimes not appropriate. African's shouldn't be under attack when one African commits a crime and one shouldn't publicly attack all Moroccans when one Moroccan commits crime. This doesn't help a nation but rather builds hatred between the foreigners and the citizens. In every country where they don't embrace foreigners, integration is poor. Many forget that better integration builds a healthy society.

It is good to learn a language to be able to communicate with the people, but it is not good for a doctor from a Third World Country trying to integrate to be forced to learn carpentry because he couldn't study in Netherlands or French. There are ways professionals from foreign origin could upgrade their careers by taking courses in English. When people from other countries get their certificates and diplomas translated in Belgium, it becomes a big problem in Antwerp. Unfortunately that doesn't help or guarantee that the person will be a doctor or engineer in Belgium. You will end up washing dishes in a restaurant because you need to pay for your accommodation and feed yourself.

The Forklift Driver

When all efforts to study journalism in Belgium seemed abortive, I had no choice but to enrol in forklift driving school. At the time, I was working as a cleaner, but I thought that getting a certificate for something could easily facilitate my employment and lead to a greater appreciation for my skills. I registered at the Flemish Public Employment and Vocational Training Service, or the VDAB, and entered into a forklift driving school at TIVO in Antwerp. I had read that forklift courses ranged from four to six weeks or sometimes only two months. My course lasted six months which was unbelievable. After passing the theory test in safety and other protective measures, I successfully had my certificates for passing my practical test on forklift, reach truck, and stapler driving.

When you compare Belgium to other European countries, Belgium is the most comfortable country to live in, but employment issue is a very difficult situation. Many European countries like Holland are choked with foreigners working as cleaners, but since it's tough to get a job in Belgium, many of its citizens are in the cleaning sector. Where I work as a cleaner, the school organises many workshops for its workers. At times the workshops teach us about the products we use or computers, so that cleaners can have knowledge on their usage.

Once, one of the Belgian women in the cleaning service inquisitively told someone that I couldn't speak good Netherlands because I fumbled with my construction of the sentences. The person she remarked to replied saying that "Joel is a foreigner and trying to speak Netherlands, you are a Belgian and can speak good Netherlands and French, yet both of you are cleaners, so you mustn't speak about people," and then she shut her mouth. Belgians have taken over the cleaning sector even more than foreigners. Sometimes it's very annoying to work with many of them, especially the ones that are addicted to tobacco. Within an hour they take more than four smoke breaks, leaving everything for you to do.

Even though I'm licensed to drive forklift, there was no permanent job for me anywhere in Belgium. I only found work at warehouses, through work agencies. Sometimes I worked three times in a week, and often there would be an entire week before I got called back in. Despite these issues, I eventually worked as a industrial forklift driver at an iron firm called Fabricom, through the cleaning company ANCCO, in Antwerp. Like many West Africans, where ever I worked, I did it wholeheartedly and with passion.

We work very hard, because we want our names to be on the list from Monday to Friday.

At Fabricom while busily working, one of my colleagues from North Africa came to me and asked if he could ask me a question. "Go on," I said. "Why are you working like a crazy man, is the work for your father? Use your brain to work. Don't kill yourself," he stated and went away. It's very confusing when someone asks you a question like that. Is he right? Am I wrong? I ignored him and went on with my work. Another time, a colleague also from North Africa asked me if I had gotten a loan at the bank. I asked him why he wanted to know. He was also displeased with the way I worked hard.

These North Africans are extremely lazy people, even though almost each one of them have full-time, permanent contracts, whilst those like me from West Africa, were without any contract. We pleaded every day for a year contract and none had it. There are always those dark days on the calendar. One day, while busily working, two of the colleagues who had been telling me that I worked too hard were caught, fast asleep in wheelbarrows. Ludo, the boss, got mad and called Ancco's boss saying "it's over my dead body if I ever I paid two of your staff caught red handed sleeping in a wheelbarrows." The workers were sent home.

In any normal world, such workers would lose their jobs right on the spot. Ancco kept them and send them to another place to work. I found out later that my colleagues from West Africa knew what was gong on. The Ancco's boss was more interested in those lazy workers than those working hard, because the delaying tactics prolonged the work which gave the company more money, while our hard working rapidly ended the job. Who says there isn't any corruption in Europe? A lot of my colleagues, including me stopped the work when we knew what was going on.

At the same Fabricom, workers lunches began to disappear without a trace. After a day of hard work, most of the workers came to the cafeteria to discover their lunch boxes stolen. This went on for several weeks and when the authorities were finally fed up, they secretly kept someone there to survey, watch, and catch the culprit. Then shortly before lunch hour, they caught the culprit. It ended up being one of my colleagues from Portugal. Ancco was called over to hear the case and the man was stopped by the Fabricom management from working there so Ancco sent him to another company to work.

The European Union: Failure or Success

Kwame Nkrumah, the first president of Ghana, formerly Gold Coast, had many major plans to transform Africa when he was elected as head of state. Apart from liberating Africa from colonial power, it was his desire to unite Africa. His dreams became a mere fantasy when he was overthrown and died in exile. As the years advanced in impoverished war torn Africa, the Organisation of Africa Union was established to help solve war problems, ethnic conflicts, and genocides. Unfortunately, the OAU didn't do enough to prevent or solve those ethnic conflicts which caused much unrest in Africa, as thousands of Africans land at European shores requesting political asylum.

The question is, "would the European Union ever be successful when the African Union has failed?" Realistically, African politics shouldn't be compared to European politics in any way because Europeans think nothing good comes from Africa apart from the raw materials that the European markets depend heavily upon. Corruption has dented African politics beyond remedy but this same corruption exists in European politics as well. It's just called a different name- "misappropriation of funds." However, at times it is necessary to compare and analyse things that take place in both Africa and Europe for the Europeans to see their failures as well.

Before the unification of Europe, Western Europe's economy, trade, and marketing were flourishing on their own currencies. The German's Deutschmarks, the Dutch's Guilders, Belgium's Franc, and other currencies were in good value and sustaining the economy without problems. Those golden years are gone and nothing could bring them back. The European Union was formed to boost the relations between the government of European countries and to strengthen trade and commerce. The members of the unified Europe then came out with one common currency, which is known as the 'Euro' today.

The problem the union faced and is currently facing is knowing that the union has brought disaster and calamity upon the member states and the economy. The reality is that the European Union has failed, as the powerful countries failed to monitor the economy of the weaker ones. Greece, Ireland, Portugal and Spain appeared to suffer most. Belgium seems a bit stronger, but they are still gradually drifting into the ocean of debt. The collapse of Dexia bank in Belgium is an example of Belgium's crumpled financial state. Dexia bank was sold to the government at four billion Euros through an investment company.

Today the bank stands as Belfius bank throughout Belgium.

The financial disaster seemed inevitable because the countries affected the worst by the financial crisis followed imprudent economic policies by spending more than they could afford. No amount of loans given to these economically troubled countries could help or alleviate the problems caused by their depressing economies because issuing loans to pay loans doesn't work. Despite the efforts to rescue them through lending schemes and the imposition of strict austerity and privatisation measures at the same time, it negatively sent them into economic protectorate for their own sake. All salvation plans turned out to be fruitless efforts and surprisingly, the last attempt to help them on December 9, 2011, was also a failure because of "the markets'" distrust and their effectiveness. The aftermath of the formation of the European Union that's taken place is brutal.

The current position of Europe is very fragile. The 27 nations all have their own economic policies and 17 of them are using the common currency, the 'Euro'. With 27 member states with different governing and direction, there is no doubt that there are going to be major problems. Many have lost their jobs, firms, or industries and gone bankrupt. Prices of commodities are twice more expensive. Many people have lost their houses because they can't pay the mortgage and the prices of renting a house has doubled in cost leaving many people homeless. The debt crisis in Europe seems to get worse and worse every day, which makes you wonder why the union was even formed.

The world has witnessed the fall of Europe's Euro and financial system. This has allowed Africans to see that Europeans are not successful in everything they do, as they may have previously thought. Could one call this a successful European Union? Not at all. There are rumours that all the countries who were bailed out will soon need another bailout. From every angle, the European Union is a total failure, since the goals on which the union was built weren't achieved. I've said that "it is better for one to take time and think where he is going, or else you may not like where you end up." The question now is what's next after the failure?

When I was ready to publish my third book, I was financially exhausted due to the bitter experiences with two bad publishers in United States of America. I lost over three thousand dollars to bad publishers who were listed on the internet as publishers in the United States of America so the money meant for the third book was used to pay the new publisher. There are many people and companies out there that believe that success requires them to operate aggressively in dishonesty but things do not work that way. Create a better name and service for your company to get more customers over cheating. Cheating creates a bad reputation for such company. A bad publisher can never survive in the publishing industry. That is the reason many publishing companies have closed down.

Many people are successful whenever it comes to fundraising but I have never been successful when looking for book sponsors. The first time I tried, no one responded after posting letters to respective people I knew because when black men ask for money, they often aren't given a second look. Rampant corruption in Africa has casted a gloomy shadow on black men, so I failed miserably which required me to sponsor the books on my own. When I successfully published my first and second book, I changed my methods of raising money to see if that would help.

I worked in a school with more than fifty teachers. I didn't want any of them to know that I had published a book, so I refrained from contacting them. I knew many of them would not respond to my request if I did give them letters so instead, I contacted two different people- the director of the school and the fashion director. Attached to a copy of the book was a letter emphasising that the book is free and I'm humbly appealing if they could assist me with any amount for my next book. The same day, I was working outside when one of the female teachers came to park her car few meters away from where I was. I stopped working and went to her. I had known this lady for almost two years now and had greeted her many times but never asked her name.

I approached her, greeted her, and asked her name. She said she was Mevrouw Pascale (Mrs Pascale). I told her that I had a book for her and wanted to know where I could leave it for her to look over. She told me to leave it at the teachers' office. When I went to the office to submit the book to her, there were many other teachers there. Many of them saw me hand over something in an envelope to her, so I quickly left to continue my work. Thirty minutes later, I returned to my boss' office and I saw the envelope I had left for Mrs. Pascale on the table with her name crossed out and mine written in its place. I was upset not only because she refused to sponsor the book, but because she refused it in an unkind manner. She didn't respond as I expected, but I took it calmly. I was aware of this attitude some Belgians possess, which is why I had initially refrained from contact any teacher.

As a teacher, I expect Mrs. Pascale to be more intelligent when deal with issues like that. I completely lost my respect for her that day. I ceased to greet her. Suddenly, I became the laughing stock, a subject of ridicule among the teachers. The rejection of my book became the new gossip for her colleagues to laugh about. It was one of the most embarrassing moments of my life. What did I do to deserve this outcome? Some teachers stuck up for me, and I felt a sort of happiness when some of the teachers denounced their co-workers negative attitude towards me.

I went to the first floor later that evening and they had grouped in one of the classrooms talking and laughing over the situation. One female teacher came out of the classroom laughing, and as soon as she saw me she retreated to tell the others that I was in the hallway. I met the fashion director downstairs and talked to her about what happened. "We have different kinds of people Joel," she said. That was the most intelligent thing I heard that day.

There are many women who think driving fancy cars and putting on the best clothes make them ladies when it really is the character of a person that matters. No one can walk on you, unless you allow them. I don't want anyone to walk on me because I am a human being who deserves respect. The respect people show me will be given back to them in the same measure. The ugly attitude those people showed to me that fateful day is something that I will never forget. I have always said that "whatever happens to me benefits me in a special way," and I have recovered to write my story. I wouldn't have anything to write about if this hadn't happened.

To be sincere, I have not felt bad for a single day for making my living cleaning in Belgium. I am very proud to be a cleaner for a simple, logical reason. Cleaners are also human beings. They deserve respect like any other human being, even though many times others will disrespect them. The idea that being a cleaner marks them as unintelligent is false. There are many cleaners who are more intelligent than many that have certificates and diplomas and serve in various institutions. Frankly speaking, I believe that those that do not respect cleaners themselves are not clean. In short, they are dirty people. People will understand and respect a cleaner more when they realize that his or her services help preventing epidemics and create healthy environment.

On Mondays, I cleaned classrooms and made them ready before school started at 8.15 A.M. The two toilets at the playground that served the male and female students were always clean. Most of the students tended to be destructive. They would deliberately mess up the toilets and as a result, we would suffer. I endured it all, keeping in mind that I had a goal to accomplish. I emptied many rubbish containers and moved around the school compound, cleaning the environment. Working hard and writing my books mean a lot to me. My books are like my trophies, awards and honours for the hard work.

At the end of the week when I was subjected to ridicule, I posted this on my Facebook page: "I had a dream about Antwerp-Tribute to Martin Luther King Jr. I had a dream that one day, I would see a black bus driver in Antwerp, and after five years I saw one in the city. I had a dream that one day, I would see a black policeman within the Antwerp police force, and after six years in the city, I saw one. I had a dream that one day, I would see a black journalist writing for the Belgian newspapers, and that dream hasn't been fulfilled yet. I had a dream that one day, I would see a black journalist appearing on the Belgium television, that dream is yet to be fulfilled. I had a dream that one day I would see what is very common in many European countries, concerning the Blackman, will also be common in Antwerp. Finally, I had a dream that one day Belgium would recover from its shock syndrome, after bitterly losing its grip on colony Congo, because that is what has caused all the bitterness against the Blackman."

After I posted this piece to the public on Facebook, that Monday at work, teachers, that I normally greeted everyday refused to respond to my greetings. What I posted has annoyed or made some of them angry. It had been only a couple of days since I had become the subject of ridicule and everyone was laughing at me because I gave my book to one of the teachers and when I thought it couldn't get worse, the posting of that article changed everything. Do they really know what pain others feel when they treat them that way? People, who like to hurt others, truly don't understand pain. The truth has paralysed them.

The truth is that the bile was too bitter to swallow. The truth, powerful as a light defeating the darkness has angered them. Who cares if you don't respond to my greetings? Those who believe I am right and do not care about what I posted on Facebook, greet first before me. I am still writing in my misery and will continue writing since I am fortunate to see the blue sky every morning through Christ who strengthens me. I don't think it would have mattered to me as a writer if I had been born without hands. My passion would have enabled me to write with my toes. Hatred doesn't pay. It's one of the cancers of society that ignites violence. I have learned how to love through my misery and not hate.

European Journalists Centre Helps African Journalists

Many people are good at hiding their problems. They pretend that their problems don't exist, even when they do. This is not just a part of Belgian culture; it's a part of culture everywhere. I don't know why some people choose to think like that, but often I wonder if it's because they don't believe they have the power to bring about change or if they simply don't like to make changes at the disadvantage of others. The International Federation of Journalists, the European Journalism Centre, and the Flemish Journalists Association never swore that they were not aware of the problems immigrants, including foreign journalists, are facing in Belgium, concerning lack of courses, workshops, and other programmes for facilitating journalism and proper integration.

I have been living in Belgium as a member of the Flemish Journalists Association for the past five years without attending any seminars, workshops, or conferences concerning my profession. Then, almost like a miracle, I received an invitation to travel Brussels. The European Journalism Centre (EJC) and the European Commission's DG Trade co-organised a two-day seminar to discuss the trade between European Union and the African Caribbean Pacific countries (ACP). The European Journalists Centre is a non-profit organisation dedicated to the highest efficiency in journalism and it trains for both African and European journalists and media professionals. The EJC has experienced journalists who promote high quality journalism and builds upon its extensive network in a wide variety of promotion of the media through professional training.

In the past archives of the European Journalist Centre, these independent journalism professionals had helped African journalists and they still do so today. They are connected to journalists worldwide and have a special website dedicated to seminars. One of these workshops and seminars was organised in Nairobi, Kenya. This programme was designed to target specifics in the country's media landscape, based on a lack of in-depth research and range of programmes on issues of development. I benefitted immensely from taking part in such a seminar. Being a participator in the seminar was the happiest day in my life because it was my first experience a journalist. The seminar also provided an overview of the current EU-ACP trade policy and an analysis of the trade limitations.

Traders from the Caribbean and the Pacific Countries who trade with the European Union believe that the new trade agreement, though compatible with the World Trade Organisation rules, was planned to the benefit of European Union. As a result, they fear affecting the economy of the ACP countries. One example of this would be the poor prices offered by the European Union. This ongoing war of trade arguments led to the seminar in Brussels. The European Journalist officials requested the publication of the outcome of the seminar. The articles I prepared were published online in *The Voice* Magazine and appeared in the newspaper 'Weekly Spectator', in Accra, Ghana.

I posted the whole copy of the newspaper which the article appeared in to the European Journalists Centre. I also wrote on exporting from Africa to Europe, since many are not used to Africa's rules and regulations. I tried many times to send articles to the Belgian newspapers but none were ever published. It wasn't because the articles were poor or below the standard of publication; they simply refused to publish the articles. Even my common letters never received replies. I can't begin to accuse the media of racism or discrimination because they know the reasons best, but I do know that this was a common problem that many African writers and journalists were facing in Europe the time because they viewed Africa as inferior.

African journalists are facing many problems in Europe because many are not in their real professions and there is no African platform or association in Europe to support them. There is a particular sports photo journalist living in Antwerp who called me to examine his work as a professional photo journalist. I was impressed and overwhelmed with the archives of his professional background. His work was broad; it spread across the entire continent. He had pictures with presidents from across the world, great football stars including Pele, the former Brazilian soccer star turned Sports Minister, George Weah, former Liberian soccer star and the FIFA boss, Sepp Blatter, CNN sports journalist, Pedro Pinto, and a host of others.

He needed my help to contact a few journalist associations to get registered. Like everyone else, he wanted better integration. I told him the reality. "Shariff, we are in Belgium and this is Antwerp, where common things regarding Blacks are not often noticed." I gave him a few addresses, including the Flemish Journalists Association address in Antwerp but his consultations yielded nothing. He ended up cleaning the streets of Antwerp, much like me. However, as I previously stated, I am the happiest man working in my profession as a cleaner. I trained myself to think that way in order to prevent depression and frustration so I could get along with my life and my passion as a writer.

African journalists in Europe face problems receiving recognition from both Europeans and unfortunately from some African government officials visiting European capitals as well. Some of them regard journalists from Africa as enemies. Why is this so? This is a crucial question that must be researched and rectified, if possible. Visiting African delegations try all they can to exclude African journalists working in the capitals they are visiting from taking part in their activities. They readily agree to the requests of white European colleagues for interviews. If you ask any minister visiting an EU capital for an interview as an African journalist, he will decline.

There have been cases in which European colleagues were sent to conduct interviews prepared by African journalists, after the initial request from the African journalists were declined. They end up answering the questions that were prepared by the very African they rejected in the first place. One African leader was visiting Berlin and his delegation refused to allow him to enter a meeting that the visiting Head of State was addressing but the reporter's camera man; who was white European was allowed to enter which shocked the cameraman.

Do we need workshops? Yes. We need them urgently for our so-called leaders visiting us here from Africa. Some of them come bowl in hand, begging for handouts from their fellow European leaders. They forget that whatever handouts are doled to them come from the taxes paid by the people working here, including the taxes of the African journalists working in Europe. In short, what I am emphasizing is that the problems faced by African journalists in Europe are created not by only Europeans but also by our fellow African, so-called leaders visiting Europe. How would they be close to an African journalist living in Europe with corruption denting their image? They fear confrontation and exposure.

There was a particular Belgian, whose name I won't mention, who was working for the "Stad Antwerpen" – City of Antwerp. I didn't know his actual position, but I knew he worked with foreigners. When a fellow African writer launched his book in Antwerp, he was responsible for all the activities to promote a successful book launch. Because of this, he was accused of helping foreigners too often and lost his job. When I heard this, I quickly made an appointment with him to find out the truth and he confirmed it citing a problem that he called a "clash of different cultures." "They don't understand, but I do, because I work with the people," he told me. I interviewed him for *The Voice* magazine. His pain and anguish led him to finally move from Antwerp to live in Brussels.

Belgium is a great country when it comes to manufacturing goods but very poor indeed in the realm of integration, especially in the Flemish communities. They try to be clever by letting everyone know that things are perfect when that isn't the case at all. How could there be good integration when a worker helping a foreigner integrate loses his job for his actions? How can one expect integration to improve when a writer is forced to become a forklift driver? How does one properly integrate when teachers, economists, and other worker's careers are completely diverted and they become masons, building constructors, plumbers, electricians, sanitary workers, and welders?

I realised these problems in the beginning and I began to develop and maintain certain principles to avoid killing my passion as a writer, which ultimately was successful. This was the reason I was able to write and publish my books, despite encountering all forms of setbacks. When I was ready to publish my first and second books, I thought I wanted them published in Europe so I wrote to many publishers there, particularly in Netherlands and Belgium. I received letters in return from some of the publishers stating that they didn't publish English books and that others in England would be ready to publish them. I wrote to four Belgium publishers as well and none of them even wrote back to say "sorry, we don't publish English books."

I don't know what kind of heart my Creator placed in my body, because things that break many people down, seem to strengthen me. Through whatever I am trying to do, no matter how many obstacles I face, I make sure to jump those hurdles. To me, it doesn't matter the circumstances I write and publish my books in. I find it very satisfying and I'm happy to publish my books while working as a cleaner. I was determined to publish my books no matter the difficulties that lie on the road and when the books were finally published in America, I sent an article on the Netherlands which I had prepared for the press to a woman who was formerly the chairperson of the Flemish journalists association, so she could go through the article to see if it needed editing before it was sent to the press.

I received mail from her claiming that she was busy and couldn't do it. Before I even sent her the article, I knew she would not do it. I did it because my wife hates when people are accused wrongly. That notion is the reason that in this modern time there are no black men serving anywhere in the print or electronic media in Belgium. However, I do know that one day things will change, even if it takes one-hundred years for that change to take place. It may be that the languages are the barrier keeping things from improving, but I have met Africans who have studied very well and are still holding some of the worst positions in society.

A couple of years ago, there weren't any blacks in Belgium's politics, but today I see posters of black people and other foreigners contesting for government seats. It doesn't matter if they win or lose. The notion of them joining other Belgium candidates in contest gives me great satisfaction because I can see the country gradually changing and the promise of one day achieving better integration. I have now spent several years as a member of the Flemish Journalists Association. In the past, I published my experience as an African immigrant and a book about music in Jamaica but the marketing of the books was so poor that I decided not to publish any book in Africa again.

In the middle of my confused state as a writer and a cleaner, I received a letter from the recognition committee of the Flemish Journalists Association asking to forward my work as a professional journalist for screening, six years after my admittance into the association. They were doing their job because that screening is a part of the committee's job: to know if their members are serving in any institutions as journalists. I printed a couple of articles that I had written on my blog and sent to them. They weren't satisfied. I received a letter from them saying that I wasn't doing enough and would be screened again in 2013. Then what happens next? I don't think I know.

One thing I dislike is when organizations like the recognition committee belittle others. Those people prey upon others intelligence in order to make them feel stupid or moronic. I wrote back to them in a very harsh tone, denouncing their letter. I asked them why I had to wait until the year 2013, saying that I needed my second screening in 2012 because nothing would change in 2013.

The truth is bitterer than bile. Ever since I wrote this letter, my relationship with the association has been very sour, but this doesn't cause me to be afraid or scared. As long as the truth had been spoken, I am satisfied. After all, we are now in a democratic era where everyone has been given the opportunity to air their views. As an immigrant, I am trying my best to learn the language, but if no one is supporting me in my career as a writer, don't try to make me feel worthless. If the help I am looking for is not coming from anyone, don't let me feel like the stupid one. The situation that transpired between the Flemish Journalists Association and me, in a country for the past twelve years haven't seen any black journalist in both the electronic and print media, was difficult.

In every thriving society, the media organisations play an important role. Without the media things would never be normal but, in the early years of my stay in Antwerp, I saw that the media had completely failed. I pointed this out to the key members of the Flemish Journalists Association which led to greater hatred towards me.

Even when a foreigner goes to the press to report what has transpired or happened to them, the stories were often not published. In principle, when someone comes to the press, a journalist serving the company should be required to listen to the complaint and investigate, confirming the information by contacting the police. The Antwerp press would rarely take those proper actions if the person was African. It was a period in which the media wasn't doing enough to discourage or reduce the problem of racism in the city. It seems that now the media has realised their mistakes and I have now noticed the best of the media. In this, I congratulate them.

For example, when I received my working permit in 2002, I went to one of the banks within a community in Antwerp with the intention of opening an account. I was shocked when the bank official told me that I needed a Belgian passport before opening one. I challenged the official but I didn't approach the case through the correct channel. I left that bank and went to the same bank in another Flemish community and the account was successfully opened. Every bank has its rules, regulations, and constitution. Therefore if one of their rules says a year's valid resident permit is not acceptable for opening an account, that rule should be maintained by the branches of that particular bank. Leaving a bank that had denied me access to open an account and successfully opening the account at the same branch in another community, showed me that there was racism and discrimination at the first bank.

I quickly sent three registered letters to the director of the mayor of Antwerp, the head of the bank where they denied me from opening the account, and an institution in Brussels which dealt with cases pertaining to racism and discrimination. The director of the bank where the incidence took place refused to write to me. What he didn't know was that I had written to an office in Brussels about the racism case. When the office swiftly took action and consulted the manager about the consequences of racial discrimination, the director who had previously refused to answer my letter, quickly wrote a letter of apology. He then wrote to the office in Brussels to tell them that he had written a letter of apology to me.

The office dealing with racial problems in Brussels wrote to me to inquire about if the bank director had really written a letter of apology to me. I confirmed the truth and the case then ended. Many people think that they have money and power to do whatever they want against people they see as lesser or weaker, but sometimes when they meet the wrong one, everything can turn against them when they are confronted by the law. For example, the following story, which never appeared in any Belgium newspaper where the case took place, surrounds the sad death of this Nigerian woman on December 9, 2005.

According to her neighbour, the deceased was praying in her apartment when another neighbour, an African married to a Belgian, called the police to come to the house to investigate the noises coming from the deceased's apartment. The police arrived and forcefully removed the woman from her home on December 2, 2005 and took her to the hospital to determine her state of mind after all of the excessive noisy behaviour. At the hospital, according to her friend who visited her, the doctor diagnosed her as having a "mental problem" and kept her at the hospital for medical observation. But the woman vehemently refused to stay at the hospital because she knew she had no mental disorder. When all her pleas were turned down, she embarked on a hunger strike and became thinner and thinner each day.

At one point she was forcefully injected by the doctor to replenish the lack of fluids into her system. An hour after the injection, she was found lifeless and all attempts to revive her proved futile. The brother of the deceased arrived in Belgium from Nigeria, when he heard of his sister's death. According to him, to the best of his knowledge there was nothing wrong with his sister. "We were communicating regularly on the phone and we would have known if she was sick or mentally disturbed," he said. According to him, before her death she was preparing to travel home to spend the Christmas holidays. "In fact when her room was opened by the police, they discovered that all her luggage packed, showing that my sister was ready to travel before her sudden death," he stated.

In a modern country like Belgium and a city like Antwerp, where the press plays a vital role in dissemination of news, how could such a serious case escape the attention of the media? If this had happened to a Belgian in Africa, it wouldn't have escaped the attention of the media in Europe, let alone Belgium, where the person came from. But because the victim was an African, her story wasn't significant enough to be published in the newspaper. I am an immigrant. Because of this, I see things differently. I respect every white man, Belgians or not, but that doesn't mean that I will praise them when things are not right. I will criticize and talk about whatever may be going wrong in society. My aim is to alert the authorities and prevent enmity and hatred in the society between foreigners and the citizens.

In the European parliaments, politicians argue, scream, yell and often fight. Security cameras have captured many of these fight scenes. What are they fighting over? Some of the politicians are not united. Others are not happy about issues like passed resolutions. Because of this, they are opposing each other. Many European journalists write against the African government and its rampant corruption and at the end of the year, that journalist may win an award for being the "best journalist of the year" for his or her contribution to better understanding of value, benefits of diversity and fight against corruption in Africa. But as an African journalist living in Europe, when I write against poor integration, racism and discrimination, I am quickly seen as a threat, enemy, and a lunatic in the society because it's practically forbidden for an African to speak against a white man.

Once I had the opportunity to interview the great South African reggae musician, Lucky Dube. He was killed in Johannesburg on October 18, 2007 by a team of gunmen who wanted to steal his car. I asked him "When you were young, do you ever dream that one day you will be such a great star to be known all over the world?" He said "Well, I had an idea. Really this was a dream for me. I wanted to be like that, even though I didn't have a clear vision as to know how big I could be. But I had an idea that I wanted to make the music reach people everywhere in the world".

This particular answer has been my inspiration in my writing career. I have met so many unfriendly characters during my time as a writer any time I needed support, but still I am writing because I have refused to let those upsets break me down psychologically and emotionally. My aim is to let my books touch people in all corners of the world as an African writer with stories that might not be found in European novels, to attract bids for foreign imprints, and someday even receive bids from movie studios. There are so many unknown writers whose hard work paved the way to them becoming bestselling authors. Like a worm trying to find its way from the underneath the ground to the surface of the earth, one day I will shine.

Meeting the Politician, Bart De Wever

The Flemish Journalists Association holds meetings and activities twice a year. In the middle of the year, a special place is chosen for the excursion and an end of the year press conference is held to select or nominate members to hold key positions in the association. When I applied for my membership, I was still learning my Netherlands, but improving rapidly. On many occasions, I could feel opposition and sense gossiping over my acceptance as a member of this association but that did not bother me a bit because I do not think you do not need to be an intelligent man to study the Flemish people.

I have said it repeatedly to other foreigners that before the Flemish will be able to do something better for us concerning integration, they first must love and cherish their own people, the Walloons. How can you expect the Flemish to love foreigners wholeheartedly when they don't even love their own neighbour? Jesus knew about mankind's problem, which was probably why he said that the greatest of all the commandments is to "love thy neighbour as thy self."

At an end of year gathering at Novotel in Antwerp, I met the Belgian-Flemish politician, Bart De Wever. Bart De Wever is a popular man when it comes to Belgian and European politics. He is the leader of the New Flemish Alliance party, N-VA. His ideology and philosophy make him a controversial person. The only person in Africa whom I could compare Wever's stances to is the late Odumegu Ojukwu of Nigeria. De Wever wants to effectively control the Flemish vital resources for economic interests. His similar desires and ideology to those of Ojukwu led to the first civil war in Nigeria, known as the Biafran war. Ojukwu wanted Nigeria to be divided into Nigeria in the West and the Biafra Republic in the East, since the greatest part of the country's resources lie in the East. This led to the war that scarred Nigeria until now.

Living and working in Belgium as a foreigner is very interesting. While I was there, I tried to learn the cause of the antagonistic relations between the Flemish and the Walloons when a woman from the Flemish Journalists Association explained that the struggle was historical. According to her, during the Second World War, the commander leading the Belgian army was a French national. Since many of the soldiers were Flemish and couldn't understand French, they couldn't follow the instructions of the French commander. He therefore ordered the execution of the Flemish soldiers. I was terribly moved after hearing this story. I consider this as one of the biggest crimes against humanity. "These are some of the reasons we hate them," she said.

Because of this, it is hard to understand Mr. Wever's desire to divide Belgium instead of burying the hatchet and building good relations with their neighbours. To many Flemish people, he would be considered the next Messiah-straitening up things in the Flemish community whenever given the opportunity. To others, particularly Walloons and some Flemish people, he is a devil in disguise because of his extreme ideas and unsolicited speeches against Wallonia. In one of his speeches, which he later apologised for, he also spoke against the Jews. Frankly speaking, I don't see Bart De Wever or Filip De Winter as bad people or racists, despite the negative perception society has given these two famous politicians.

Every country has its rules, laws, and regulations to follow. That's probably the reason that we often hear "When in Rome, do what the Romans do." As leaders, they loved their country. They tackled the roots of the problem to build a better future for the country, but weakened the foundation at the same time. Because of this, many do not agree with them. For instance, a Christian can never go to any Islamic country to ask for permission to build a church. You are not only going to be denied that permission, but you will also end up in prison for speaking out about Christianity in an Islamic country. Yet the Moslems want to build

Mosques in every part of Europe, even though thousands already exist. When anyone opposes them, they call that person a racist. This doesn't make sense.

When Mr. Filip De Winter, the leader of the "Vlaamse Belang" party, stepped into the picture, campaigning against crime and other social vices committed by foreigners in the city of Antwerp, many called him a racist. The leader of the "Vlaamse Belang" party is following the right course of bringing sanity to his dear country, but the 'aggressive' way he does it puts many people in fear. It was this same foreigners issue that made the American Embassy in Brussels deny him an invitation to attend President Obama's inauguration in 2009. Despite this, the man is not as bad as many thought.

At one point, people turned against Bart De Wever for being a racist man with an unhealthy mind concerning his political stances. Once, when being interviewed on a morning television programme in 2008, Mr. Wever made a shocking statement.

"I think that there are no French-speaking minorities in Flanders; the immigrants have to adapt," he said. "We asked the Moroccans and the Turks to do that. We didn't say to them 'There are a lot of you, so Arabic will become an official language.' That's crazy."

Meeting Bart De Wever at a Flemish Journalists Association meeting was a good opportunity to listen to him. I had listened to many of his interviews, but that isn't the same as hearing him in person. I could now behold this controversial man myself. I didn't ask him any questions, but I did enjoy the questions many of my colleagues threw at him. De Wever had an answer to every question he was asked. At one point, he explained the usage of Dutch as the sole language in government agencies and integration. This to me didn't make sense. Why should Mr. Wever advocate for the usage of Flemish in offices throughout the provinces, when three official languages are spoken in the country?

The interesting thing is the language he was advocating was the result of poor integration between the Flemish and the Walloons. If that was the case, then I am right to say that there is poor foreign integration in Antwerp. If it becomes better, then one day the Flemish and the Walloons relationship might also be better. The question is when. After the conference, I asked if one of my colleagues could take a picture of Mr. Wever and me. He accepted. I had kept the picture of Mr. Wever and me for a very long time, until one day when I posted it on my Facebook page before he won the election as the mayor of Antwerp. After the posting, I began receiving negative comments, the first coming from a Belgian woman who accused me of collaborating with a man she called "sick."

According to her, Mr. Weaver made things difficult for her mother when they lived in Wallonia. I received more negative feedback and every accusation and hostility remark waged against Mr. Wever was based on his political views and opinions.

The second of these attacks came from an African. He attacked me verbally, calling me a traitor for collaborating with Bart De Wever. I ignored all the attackers, for the most part, but I did post this: "I don't see or have any reason to hate Mr. Wever. He was at the Flemish Journalists Association meeting and I requested to take picture with him and he accepted. If there is any need to hate people then the hate should go to Adolph Hitler and the leaders of Apartheid and those who supported it, including Margaret Thatcher."

Bart de Wever was once a heavy man. Criticism from the media was not only centred on his political views, but also on his weight. After this, he followed a strict diet, which transformed him into the real man he wanted to be.

In the recently concluded elections, his slogan "The power for a change" helped defeat the other candidates, including the former mayor Patrick Janssens, and he emerged as a the new Mayor of Antwerp. Quickly after his election, he called on the French-speaking Belgian prime minister Elio Di Rupo to give more rights of self-rule to the Flanders. He remarked that "We want to give

Flanders the government they want at all levels. That is why I call on Elio Di Rupo and the Francophone politicians. Take your responsibility and work for more regional autonomy."

Mr. De Wever has pledged to work for bigger gains for separatists at the 2014 national elections.

African Children in European Schools: Are They Losing their Culture and History?

With increasing numbers of people migrating into culturally diverse European schools, there is a need to see if African children in European schools are losing their culture and history. As an African child at school, we were forced to learn about Europe under the cane of our merciless teachers. We learned about wheat from Canada, coffee from Brazil, wool from Australia, the royal family in England, the Buckingham Palace, and the four seasons of Europe in geography lessons when the African children really should be studying to be doctors, engineers and other professionals.

Discipline is a rudimentary ingredient in all aspects of human life. African children usually don't lack discipline because the parents do not spare the rod and spoil the child. Culture plays an important role in the society African children grow up in. Culture is like a teacher, implanting knowledge in the child to help them identify evil and good things in the society as they grow. Recently, my research has revealed that an African child is happier in Africa than in any other country in Europe or the United States, despite Africa's lack of best educational facilities and also showed significantly more respect to school authorities and teachers than did European students.

In European schools, one can see the decline of respect, dignity and morality in children. Students continue to disrespect teachers. Many are very rude and their behaviour is sometimes shocking. Many students lack discipline because they aren't aware of what they are thinking, speaking or acting. There is a lack of discipline from the classroom to outside where teachers may not know of their obscure behaviours. At the school playground, there are dustbins everywhere, yet many children like to dump their waste on the ground. Those unaware of what they were doing quickly apologise when questioned and still others will simply tell you that "there are cleaners in the school." Rubbish is littered everywhere and sometimes you will see fruits like apples and food packaging in the toilets.

Emigration into the European society has caused African children to adopt some of these immoralities, which brings conflicts, arguments, and worries to their parents at home. Many African parents are now facing difficulties with controlling their children in Europe when their kids blindly copy European culture. These are some of the issues that have led hundreds of fathers of Islamic background to committing serious crimes. In Britain, a strict Kurdish Muslim cut the throat of his sixteen year old daughter because he thought society had westernised her into a wayward daughter. Before her death she wrote to her father "Me and you will probably not understand each other, but I am sorry there are things you can't change."

Even though her father can't understand because of his deeply inclined religious beliefs, she is right. Islam is a religion that one must be careful of speaking against. Author Salman Rushdie knows best that currently the Muslims themselves are degrading Islam. In November 2012, the 'Jerusalem Post' reported on a gay French-Algerian man, planning to open the first gay mosque in France. This came as a shock to many Muslim communities throughout the world and some thought that Islamic leaders impose a death warrant on this Algerian-French national since the Koran doesn't encourage homosexuality. Others wondered if it was necessary at all for Ayatollah Khomeini to impose the death warrant on Rudshie, when it seems that the commission of this gay mosque in France has defiled Islam more than anything else.

Following Western culture, an African child at sixteen now can bring his boy or girlfriend home to introduce to his or parents. This doesn't exist anywhere in Africa, because there it's considered a gross disrespect to the parents. That is the reason it is very common to see many people over sixteen to twenty still virgins in Africa. In Europe, on the other hand, a sixteen year old child thinks she is ripe of age and capable of having sex. Europeans may be very intelligent in many things but they should learn a few things from Africa in this area. Despite the bad economy and poor nutrition, children do not commit suicide in Africa while the rate of children committing suicide in Europe and America is on the rise. Also, despite the daily hassle and hard living in Africa, African children don't smoke but today in Europe it is a common sight to see a mushroom of teenage smokers everywhere.

It is estimated that about three thousand children smoke their first cigarette each day. That statistic doesn't exist anywhere in Africa. Teenage pregnancy is also rarely heard of in Africa, yet Europe, especially Britain now booms with teenage pregnancy. Britain has the highest rate of teenage pregnancy in Western Europe, despite having the best education program on this subject and it is estimated that one million teen pregnancies are recorded in the United States alone. How could Africa, a continent in which many lack education, are able to prevent teenage pregnancy, smoking, and other social vices, while Europe and the United States of America can't control teenage pregnancy and smoking even though they have some of the best educational facilities in the world?.

Discrimination is a factor that probably affects African children in European schools, but I don't dwell on it as an issue that would prevent them from knowing about their culture and history. Subjects exist at a broader level at school and studying Africa alone isn't enough. An African student in Africa geographically and psychologically will know much more about advanced countries but only a few whites know things about Africa. When Africa is mentioned to a European, nothing other than poverty, sickness, disease, and corruption will come to mind. The lack of teaching on African issues has affected most African children in European schools. At the school where I worked, many Africans liked to talk to me. The white students talked to me too, but the questions the African children ask me are different from the ones whites ask me.

Once, an African student between the ages of fourteen and fifteen asked me where I came from. I answered and asked her the same question. "Congo," she replied. "Do you know Patrice Lumumba?" I asked. She screamed with laughter saying "I don't know who he is."

It's sad for a girl her age to have no knowledge of Patrice Lumumba as the first premier of her country, which was colonised by Belgium, the country where she was being educated. Many African children growing up in Europe are afraid to visit Africa to prevent death by some strange disease and sickness. This is brainwashing through education.

To intensify and facilitate the quality of education, modern technology has brought many new prospects to the market including the computer. The internet connects us to any part of the world within seconds and every answer to our question is answered within a second. Every business, all travel plans, and almost everything else can be done now through the internet. But how has this polluted the mind of our children? The greed for money and the thirst for fame have prompted people to do sick things which adversely affects our children. Porno Stars and some celebrities have polluted the internet without remedy. Some celebrities now don't put on underwear and deliberately open their legs to show their hairy or shaved private parts to the paparazzi. What kind of world are we living in and how do these people not have any shame?

Young girls are copying what some celebrities and models do. Some don't want to eat. The fear of getting fat finally leads them to anorexia, in bad cases turning some of them into the living dead. Almost every commercial advert on the telly is using sex to sell, without any care if children are watching or not. We need to accept the fact that we are now in a very wrong world where many are raising disobedient children who think they know better than their parents. The internet, computer and the television might be successful inventions to facilitate education but they have adversely affected the moral behaviours of children.

Education, in the general sense, is key to future development and one of the most powerful instruments for reducing poverty. I believe this imparting of knowledge should be shared equally but not partially. African children in European schools and their European counterparts should know much more about Africa. It is a fact not an exaggeration that less is thought about Africa in European schools, where they only speak of poverty, sicknesses, diseases, corruption, crime and slavery. There are hundreds and thousands of historical and interesting facts which are worthy to be taught in advanced countries' schools.

Lightning Source UK Ltd.
Milton Keynes UK
UKOW07f0116181114

241764UK00014B/264/P